Telling It
Like It Is

DEDICATION

To Arnold, Rachel, and David
For so much love, support, and rich material;

For my sisters everywhere, but especially Ina;

And with special affection to Pat, Sue, Nancy, Jean, Barbara, Valerie, Pam, and all the others whose wanting to read more kept me writing.

CONTENTS

PREFACE

Many years ago, when I was young and on my first visit to Europe, a dashing Turk told me, on a Venetian vaporetto heading for Lido, "You make me feel so alive!" Long afterward, a much respected male colleague said of me, "If you really want to know how things are, ask Elayne. She's the only one who tells it like it is." I considered at the time—and I still do—that those were the two best compliments any man had ever paid to me.

There is, of course, nothing inherently male-female in either remark. Each of us could validate our best friend by saying the same thing. And validation is what the reflections in this collection are about.

I hope that by "telling it like it is" for me in these writings—the closest I have come to keeping a writer's journal—other women, and men, will "feel alive" and in touch with their own truths and their unique realities.

After all, no writer could ask for a better compliment—from anyone.

ACKNOWLEDGMENTS

I am enormously indebted to the following friends and colleagues for their encouragement and assistance:

Kristin Cooney, whose editorial and production skills were as constant as her good humor;

Maggie Huff-Rouselle, for her generous support and technical assistance in preparing this manuscript;

Sara Eyestone, for the gift of her art, and her spirit;

Sandy Brown and Rita McCullough of KIT Publications. Would that all writers had such a joyous association with their publishers.

And with special gratitude to Violeta Sanchez, who cooked so that I could compose.

SIGNIFICANT OTHERS

UNDER THE WILLOW TREE

When I was small, the childhood classic *Wind In The Willows*, with its gentle and whimsical characters, was by far my favorite. I think it was because of my willow tree—the weeping giant by Belle Tract Lake under which my grandmother used to tell me a "bubbachka" when she came to visit us on alternate weekends.

The ritual began with my "zoftik" bubbe walking slowly—ever more laboriously—up the street towards our house, having disembarked from the number 47 bus which had brought her from Philadelphia to our home in New Jersey. She would carry the smallest of bags with only one change of clothes, and some "chachkas" for my sister, brother, and me. When she greeted us, only the moist twinkle in her eye betrayed her reserve, as she puffed slightly from her walk, never perspiring. Her flowered dress with its lace collar and cameo brooch, covered always by a drab cardigan, smelled of a mixture of talcum powder, cigarette smoke, old newspapers, and new handkerchiefs—an odd potpourri of her own scents mingled with those of the bus which had brought her.

"Bubbe's here! Bubbe's here!" we would shout to my mother, who was already preparing Bubbe a cup of tea. The two of them would settle at the kitchen table and before long—as predictably as Bubbe's visit itself—one would say something to outrage the other, and a Yiddish shouting match of outstanding proportions would ensue, with no one the winner and both contestants exhausted, guilty and privately repentant. Then Bubbe would go to her room to rest. By dinnertime, all would be forgiven. Bubbe would bring out the "chachkas" from her tattered bag, and we would be treated to a detailed update of the trials and tribulations (not to mention the mitzvahs) of all

our cousins, aunts, and uncles in Philly. I never knew what it
was my mother argued with her mother about, and I don't
think it mattered. The only really important thing was the ritual
of rage between them, symbiotic and silly though it was.

On Sundays, if the weather was good, one of us kids would
invariably suggest, with great gaiety and originality, that we
should "make a picnic" and go to the lake—all as pretense, of
course, to hearing a "bubbachka" under the willow tree. I
don't know why they never worked anywhere else, but they
didn't. A "bubbachka" lacked all magic, all credibility, all
romance, if told anywhere else but under that mournful, ma-
jestic, weeping willow. It was also an unspoken truth that
"bubbachkas" only wove their spell if no grown-ups went
along (except for Bubbe, of course, but she wasn't a real grown-
up or our mother wouldn't have shouted at her). In silent
collusion we would prepare the picnic lunch, while Bubbe
protested that she had told us already all the "bubbachkas"
she knew the last time we went to the willow tree—loving all
the while our pleading with her to tell them again.

The picnics, like the "bubbachkas," were always the same:
peanut butter and jelly sandwiches, carrot and celery sticks,
graham crackers, and fruit juice in a red plastic container.
"Once upon a time, in a shtetl in Vilna, there was a (boy called
Jacob) (girl called Sarah) . . ." As an entourage, we never changed
either. My older sister would carry the brown grocery bag of
food. (Jewish families didn't have nice picnic baskets, no matter
how many picnics they went on. Wicker was for goyim.) My
younger brother, his nubby knees sticking out of his short
pants, would hold Bubbe's hand in an effort to keep up. And
I, in respect of my ordinal position, marched somewhere in the
middle. At the corner of Delaware Street, I became the Safety
Patrol, nodding solemnly with the all-clear to proceed. We
must have looked like a Norman Rockwell parody of the all-
American immigrants.

Miraculously, no one else ever sat under our willow when we
wanted it. Both pigeon and pedestrian respected our sacred
turf, at least on Sundays when Bubbe came. We would settle

down to feast and fable, until suddenly, prompted by the rustling of swaying willow boughs, one of us would jump up to announce that if we didn't get back, Bubbe would miss her bus back to Philadelphia. A unanimous groan would accompany the hasty clean-up effort, while Bubbe promised to finish the "happily ever after part" when she returned in two weeks.

And so it was, until I was seven, and Bubbe died.

Where I live now, a huge and solitary willow tree sways nearby in an empty horse paddock. I cannot pass it without remembering, and hearing "the wind in the willows." I haven't gone to sit under it yet. But one day, when I am a Bubbe, I will. I will gather my grandchildren to me, and I will tell them a "bubbachka." It will be about my grandmother, who came "once upon a time, from a shtetl in Vilna, and whose name was Brona . . ."

bubbachka - a tale told by grandparent
zoftik - hefty
chachkas - trinkets
mitzvah - joyous occasions, blessings
shtetl - village
goyim - Gentiles

WRITING MY MOTHER'S LIFE

"**I** want you to have my typewriter," she said from her nursing home bed.

Not "Take my typewriter." As in "Take my pictures. I won't need them anymore. Take my jewelry. Take my good coat."

This time she said "I want you to have my typewriter." I heard the difference, and it was deafening, and this time, I took the typewriter.

Soon after, she said, "I want you to write the story." By the time she told me this, "the story" in her mind was about the nurses poisoning her and conspiracies of cruelty and eviction. I promised to tell the story: not that one, of course, but her real story.

I have known for a long time that I needed to tell the story of my mother. I have needed to do it so that I could reconcile her life, and in so doing, could begin to put an end to fear and great sadness. At first I thought I would have to gather many more facts. I would go in search of a great oral history, I thought, and in her roots and her childhood I would discover my mother and would come to make sense of her life.

But in my mind it was still one life—one story to be told. Now I know that is why I could not begin: because the telling of my mother's life is two stories, and the cruelty of that reality is that the two can never be reconciled.

The first story is a fiction, and it contains the facts. It begins with a female child being born in 1904 to Russian Jews somewhere in eastern Europe, close to, but preceding, the High Holy Days of Rosh Hashana; so that her birthday was celebrated on August 25 each year. Her Hebrew name was Brona, but she chose to be called Reba as she grew up in small town, anglicized New Jersey to which she had emigrated at the age of two. Her father—a tailor—was distant while she grew up, but her mother—for whom she felt an almost painful love—was devoted. They were friends, which was a great tragedy for my mother in the end. There were also two brothers.

Reba, a good student, went from eighth grade straight to secretarial school, where she excelled. After graduation, she worked as a legal secretary to "Pepper, Bodine, Stokes and Shock," until Mr. Bodine, who was old enough to be her father, chased her around the office one day with a strand of real Parisian pearls and a litany of promises.

I can understand his devotion: My mother was a real beauty. While I was growing up, I cherished the photograph of her swathed in pastel blue and pink, her large dark pools of eyes peering mysteriously out from under the frame of rich black curls which she later had bobbed. (Her mother would not speak to her for three weeks. Then she had her hair bobbed as well.) My mother must have been about 18 years old in that picture, but other, later photographs were equally stunning. In one, wearing green satin and velvet lounging pajamas, she looked just like a young and glamorous Indira Gandhi; in another, at the Chicago World's Fair in 1936, she is the epitome of New York chic in a black suit and saucy hat dipped over one eye. My mother had true class.

She was also talented, energetic, full of humor and high hopes—everybody's dream girl—which is why she began to contribute to her own fiction.

In her brilliant book, *Writing A Woman's Life*, Carolyn Heilbrun—to whom I am deeply indebted for helping me to understand (and tell) my mother's story—explains the fiction of women's lives and of their autobiographies. Gertrude Stein, Jane Austen, and Eudora Welty wrote fiction as autobiography because they had not the language, nor the forum, nor even the perception of their own lives to write with truth for public consumption. The essence of their own experience, recorded—if at all—only in private letters and journals, had no place in traditional accounts of female lives. No language existed in the male experience or in the male paradigm of literature or life to allow for the diversity, ambition, or passion of women's lives. Traditional accounts and conventional chronicles of women were built upon layers of concealment and closure. Women had therefore to find beauty in pain, and to make of their rage spiritual acceptance, becoming, in the final analysis, female impersonators. My mother neither wrote, nor lived, her own life for the very same reason. Instead, she tried vigorously and with valor to be the best of impersonators.

She waited at first, continuing, I believe, to know somewhere in the recess of her heart and her intellect that there was more. With no language to express it, no literature to validate it, no friend with whom to explore it, she put away her dreams, her aspirations, her intellectual curiosity. Finally, at the age of 36, she gave up ideas of leaving her needy mother for a career in New York. She no longer believed in adult love as she had dared to imagine it. She began instead to embrace myth, which is why—as Carolyn Heilbrun knows—the telling of women's lives has always ended with marriage and children. When, in her passivity, my mother married a man she should not have, and began a life she did not really want, she did not even question the emptiness of having it all; although, of course, she did find great joy in her three children, to whom she was the greatest of mothers.

Later, no longer able to sustain what was forbidden to her—anger, the desire for power and control over her own life—and unable to find a voice in which to publicly complain or privately comprehend, she began—like millions of other women who take themselves to be the only one—to take refuge in depression, which, in the end, became lucid madness, inherent in which was a terrifying power, pervading her presence like bitter irony in a tasteless joke.

It didn't happen all at once. In between the "bad spells" there were some good moments: the joy of working in my father's haberdashery at Christmastime, trips to Florida and Canada, the laughter of children, and the ceremonies of life. She took joy in her grandchildren, with whom even a McDonald's hamburger was a cherished treat. She loved writing great long letters full of humorous anecdotes and colorful detail. "I'm going to start a book!" she would say, pulling out her Smith-Corona portable. But those moments were not many in the whole fabric of her life. She deserved more—much, much, more.

She did not deserve to be incarcerated in institutions designed and run by men who saw in women's depression only depravity and not longing, diversity, and depth. She did not deserve to have electrodes put to her head so that in the end she could not remember the dates of her children's birthdays. She did not deserve meaningless labels like "involutional melancholia," and "manic-depressive," and "bi-polar disorder." She did not deserve in her old years to become ugly—even grotesque—and crazy and difficult to be with because of the perversities of her life.

These are not easy things to say about your mother—or to remember—but they must be said and remembered, because they are true and the truth about women's lives must be told.

My mother's life had another truth that can be told only in another story, which we must come to recognize and cherish (for many women) as unrealized biography.

In that story, my mother has the same chance beginnings. But the childhood passion which is female, and Russian, and unique to her as well, is nurtured like a seedling from whose sprouting the whole world will be fed. She is encouraged, like her brothers, to study, to "make something" of herself. She is rewarded for independence, action, curiosity. Her budding world view is encouraged, even if it can only be in New York. Her desire to delay marriage for travel and career (to try being a writer?) is not frowned on or laughed at; and her successes—small though they may be—are cause for excitement and celebration, not restricted to wedding receptions and a "bris" insofar as women are concerned.

When she grapples with the essence of female experience, or the human dimensions of anger, grief, fear, or uncertainty, there is a feminist community to share it, to say, "You are not alone," and to serve as midwife to the birth of spirit. No surgeon tries instead to excise it as if it were an aberrant growth because it only grows in women. Later, when she marries, it is with the joy and maturity of friendship and the sensuality of full being. She continues to work; not as handmaiden to her husband, but as fullbodied self in whatever realm she chooses. She is devoted to, but not defined by, her children. She takes pleasure in a McDonald's hamburger with her grandchildren, but she feels worthy of dinner at Maxim's. She grows old with intellectual and physical elegance (which does not mean she is still slender). Her mind is clear, she is still a woman of taste and vision; and when she lets go, it is not out of defeat, or defiance: it is the letting go of peaceful demise, knowing that life, in all its richness, has been hers not by chance, but by the design of a life self-determined and well-lived.

This unrealized biography, and not the fiction of my mother's life, is the story I promised to tell and that those of us who love my mother, who is Everywoman, must celebrate. It is the one she always meant to write, on her typewriter and on her palette of possibility.

It is the life she deserved to live.

ON MOTHER'S DAY . . . TO MY DAUGHTER . . .

This is a day which traditionally dictates that you lavish attention on me. But it's also a chance for me to take stock, from the other side of the relationship, of our 17 years together. As I think about it, I feel pretty lavish myself.

I'll never forget the day you were born. I'd had a lovely pregnancy: you were easily conceived, carried with grace (or did I just imagine I was Madonna?), and delivered naturally in very short order. You emerged, turned your pink face upward for a good look, and announced heartily that you were here to stay. From the very beginning you fit nicely into my life. You were a good nurser, an excellent traveler, and a charming guest. In time, you outgrew the first of these virtues; the other two remain to your credit.

I knew early that you were going to be bright and precocious. But it took a while longer to realize your determination, which emerged during your "first adolescence"—the Terrible Twos. What a shock! Toddlerhood is overwhelming to a mother, because suddenly we face the awesome responsibility of having another personality dependent on us, and frightening because with stark reality we confront our own inadequacy and needs. No one really prepares us. We only know, unconsciously, that as good mothers we must subordinate our own desires to those of our child. We don't really know how to handle our anger, frustration, and guilt—so often born of fatigue. The only thing we are sure of is our unequivocal and bottomless love; that tugging at the heart that goes all the way to our toes when a pair of trusting eyes twinkle, "I love you, Mom."

So there you were, viewing the world from its center, which you took to be your rightful place. And there I was, floundering to meet the demands of this very distinct personality—yet, in so many ways, the mirror of my own. There were times, and still are, when I see myself so clearly in your actions, your expressions, your judgments. I watch you struggle to cope with disappointment and it is me. I see your quick wit, and I recognize my own girlhood. I witness your compassion, and I feel my own pain. You thrust a hip, grin, gesticulate, and uncannily, you are me.

Is it in this mirror image that our conflicts lie? Are we so alike that we reflect not only the best, but also the worst, of each other? And if that's true, is it really so bad? Oh yes, we can be driven to profound rage; hurt to the essence of our souls; guilty beyond reason. That passion is played out precisely because we are safe with each other: because we know that the bonds of love, trust, and loyalty between us can never be broken, we can do our growing together. We can flourish, fail, be afraid, take pride, because no matter what, we know that we are grounded in each other's likeness and love. At the end of every day, regardless of what it has brought to each of us, there is security in our still-present bedtime ritual. When I tuck you in and kiss your cheeks, you know what is real in the world. And when you sing out "Love you, Mom," I know too.

There is less tension now, as you grow towards womanhood, and we come together on more equal ground. We are becoming friends, and I'm glad. I like you. When we talk things over—intimate, funny, sad, confusing things—I feel deeply satisfied. I'm proud of your emerging intellect, touched by your growing world view, delighted by your sense of humor. There is deep and abiding joy for me as I watch your potential develop, your sensitivity heighten, your spirit become strong. I know, with a mother's conviction, that you can achieve whatever you put your heart and your mind to, and that your future is bright with promise. Not because I'm your mother, and not even because you're my daughter, but because you are uniquely you. And it is that which makes this Mother's Day especially mine, and why I have chosen this moment to tell you that truly, and oh so deeply, "I Love You."

                                                              Mom

"Now I Lost My Ina"

The thing I always remembered best about visiting my Aunt Tilly in my toddler years was the drawer I slept in. My mother would announce that we were going to the house on Richmond Street and I would burst with anticipation, knowing that "Aunt Tooty"—as I called her then—would have pulled out the bottom drawer of the huge armoire "from the old country" and padded it with comforters and pillows so that I could crawl into my special nest when we arrived.

But what my Aunt Tooty liked to tell about years later when we looked back on those days was how I followed my beloved older sister around. "Give a look," she would say to the other adults, in Yiddish, as I waddled after my miniature role model like a duck following its mother. "She won't let her out of sight!' And as long as my sister was there, I was calm and happy, no matter how long we stayed away from home. Only when I lost sight of her would I wail inconsolably, Aunt Tooty said, sobbing "Now I lost my Ina!" until she would reappear, grinning broad reassurance.

❧

The room we shared in the house my father built in 1950 was light and airy, and wonderfully fragrant on those spring days when the windows were first opened. My half was always picture-perfect neat, hers a profusion of clutter which began modestly enough on Mondays and reached utter disaster by Fridays. It was here that she would dress for dates every weekend while I watched and longed to be as popular one day. And it was in that room that I waited for her return every Friday and Saturday night so that she could tell me about the clever things she had said, how she had charmed her way into, or out of, situations I could only begin to imagine.

This was the place in which she told me "the facts of life," explaining why my Catholic friend's mother kept on having babies, and how my aunt and uncle, who didn't really love each other, could still "do it."

And this was the room that grew so empty and quiet and disturbingly uncluttered in 1956 when she went to college so far away that she only came back on holidays. Now I lost my Ina, I thought, for the first time since I was four years old.

🙋

On my 13th birthday, I flew for the first time in my life, alone. It was an Eastern Airlines turbo-jet and in those days (as my Aunt Tooty would have said) unaccompanied minors, and terrorists, were still a rarity, so once we departed Philadelphia and were safely on top of cotton clouds that only God could have woven, I was invited into the cockpit, where for my benefit the pilot "buzzed" Princeton stadium and a few other sites.

When my sister greeted me in Boston I was flushed with excitement, barely noticing the boyfriend she introduced me to. He seemed a minor part of the four days we spent together. What captured my imagination was going to real college classes like Greek Mythology (where I impressed my sister's friends with my limited knowledge of the Oedipus story); hearing the Boston Symphony; living in a dormitory (where everyone said "Isn't it wonderful you're so close!"); and even having a real "date" (with a good friend who knew how to make a 13-year-old happy).

So a few months later, when my sister announced that she was "pinned" to the boy in Boston, I was surprised but happy for her, even though I couldn't explain the funny feeling in my stomach. The following year, she had her ring; and suddenly it was 1958 and we were in our room getting dressed for the wedding and running through my mind was the involuntary refrain: Now I lost my Ina.

🙋

Sibling rivalry is riddled with ironies. While my sister settled into suburbia with Dr. Seuss, I spent the 1960s exploring Europe, working in New York and London, and falling in love with all the wrong men. We were wildly jealous of each other's greener grass.

Eventually I caught up. Two kids, two cars, one mortgage. We even lived in opposite suburbs of the same city. But something had happened. Some intangible, palpable, unspoken, villainous force had found its way into our lives, cutting between us like a great Diaspora.

It is not difficult to explain or accept that we became different people, made disparate life choices, and had in some ways divergent values; that we became emotional strangers is. I had, of course, my own theories, my own stories to tell, as surely, she had hers. The sad thing is that we never told them to each other; reconciliation requires such risks.

Instead, we were polite and sent birthday cards and inquired after each other at appropriate intervals and looked after our mother and suffered our mutual loss silently and alone. And in all those years, my heart never stopped aching with having lost my Ina.

With anyone else, I probably would have been the first one to suggest gently that a scan might be in order to rule out "anything to worry about." But she was so certain that it was only optic neuritis, and besides, brain tumors and aneurysms only happen to other people.

When news of the surgery came, I was, ironically, in Boston. There was never a longer journey home.

We were all there: brother, sister, daughters, spouse, surrounding her with manic humor and heroic love, none more funny than she, with her own special brand of sarcasm.

"It will be all right," I said in pedestrian prayer, anything else inconceivable. But in the end it was not alright, and on March 3, 1990, peacefully, without farewell, now and forever, I lost my Ina.

In the end there were few regrets, no *mea culpas*, little guilt. Those emotions are not big enough to touch the unspeakable loss and the grievous void. Instead, only sadness; huge, profound, heaving sadness that fills my being and stretches into my soul: for courage lacked, friendship lost, love unspoken, but ever felt.

"You're a remarkable family," the doctor said to me one night. But he never knew the half of it. Only we knew the forces that shaped us, that gave us our strength, our loyalty, our primal devotion. That was ours, only ours. And it was all that mattered, nothing else. That is what death teaches you.

That history, that sororial bond, that essence, is what binds me now to her, whom I have loved so deeply, so long. When I see flashes of her face before me, always smiling, left eyebrow sardonically raised, it is that common past, that communion, that empathy which needs no apology, no explanation, no confession. And when, in the course and kindness of time, I can remember her beyond the flashes, with wide and expansive memory, in magic moments of youth most of all, it will be with vivid, joyful connection and spirited sisterhood.

Then will I know once more, in my twilight as in my dawn, that now and forever, I have found my Ina.

TRADITION

When Zero Mostel as the rancorous Tevye in "Fiddler on the Roof" first sang of tradition, who among us did not respond to the spirited reminder of what is important in life? Yes! we said in affirmation as he stamped his foot to call attention to rituals, no matter what they might be for each of us.

Between basting the turkey and greeting the guests, I stop each year at Thanksgiving and Christmas (and again at Passover as I roll the matzo halls) to contemplate the place of tradition in my life, and to relish its gifts and its memories.

Most of the tradition I celebrate with my family did not begin in the house where I grew up, but in the home and hearts of very special people who nurtured me when my own family could not. I was officially their babysitter; at least that's how the relationship started. But they became much more to me than just neighbors, especially the mother, whom I wished desperately to be like when I grew up, got married, and had children. Helen was warm and welcoming to everyone who came into her daily life, even the vegetable man.

"Hi, Helen! Anything today?"

"No thanks, Dan. I think I'm okay," she would say, looking over her shoulder from the kitchen sink as she peeled potatoes.

"Got some nice green beans today. And some real special tomatoes!"

Before I knew what had happened, Dan was delivering an order the size of a small green grocery shop.

"He's so nice," Helen would say, "I hate to say no to him."

Every day after school, I would head over to that house, under some pretense or other, until I finally gave up pretending I had a reason—other than just wanting to be there, where warmth and love hung about like a great invisible shawl that wrapped itself around me. I would play with the kids, or sit at the kitchen table as Helen prepared her dinner; and each evening when her husband came home and kissed her, I watched with adolescent envy, and vowed to live my adult life in exactly the same way.

I haven't, of course—not exactly. But the traditions of that home have become in large measure those of my own family, from the miniature marshmallows on the sweet potatoes at Thanksgiving to the green bean casserole. We bake our Christmas cookies with Helen's recipe each year, and it is her decorations that inspire our own. When we play carols, they are, in large part, reminiscent of the spirit of her holiday home, and on Christmas eve, when we steal downstairs to lay the gifts under the tree and leave Santa milk and cookies, I remember the years when I was included in that ritual for her children.

Now, because of my own children, we are creating new traditions—ceremonies to be passed on and added to in years to come. Thanks to their British dad, we also bring the traditions of England to our holiday meal: Christmas pudding complete with brandy butter, crackers torn apart with fervor to discover fortunes and trinkets wrapped in paper hats, mince pies. And from their Jewish mother come the stories of Chanukah at this special time of year, as we light the candles of the menorah and pass out the "gelt."

Caveats and covenants, reassuring in their regularity, are obeyed year after year. For my family they include a certain table cloth, the best china and silver, and a set menu. We are never, never allowed to accept an invitation to be elsewhere on these holidays (which means, I hope, that my children will always come home, no matter where they are). And whether they have eaten or not, we must always, always bake cookies and have on the table sweet potatoes with marshmallow and green bean casserole. There will never be a Thanksgiving in my home without pumpkin pie, or a December 25 without Christmas pud; and on both occasions, when my husband pauses to give thanks, there will never be a year in which I do not go all teary, even though I know it is coming.

For others, the rituals may be quite different, and nowhere is it written that "family" must consist of Mom, Dad, two kids, two cars, one dog, and a mortgage, a la Norman Rockwell. Family is whoever we love, home is wherever they are, and tradition is what we make it, once it has shaped us.

Tevye, for all his irascibility, knew that much about life, which, I suspect, is why he kept singing.

gelt - candy coins

In Memoriam

F irst there was Gilda Radner, whom I didn't know personally, of course. Then my friend Jo Burke in England. And
then Rose Kushner, former colleague and feminist ally. Their
deaths from virulent cancers partial to women came close
together, hitting me hard, for each of them had touched me in
a special way.

They had far more in common than cancer. Each of them
lived with tenacity and vigor. Intensely private, they nonetheless
participated fully in life, giving it everything they had. Percep-
tive and fully aware of life's ironies and injustices, they were
each, in their own way, very funny women.

Gilda was the kind of woman who feels like your best friend,
even if you'd never laid eyes on her outside of a TV screen.
There was something about her insane exaggeration and parody
that told it like it was—something that validated our own perceptions about the world around us. Her outrageous acts were
so much more than comedy: they were social commentary. She
was "real people." The kid you grew up with who "did good"
and made something of herself.

My recollection of Jo, who like Gilda died in her 40s, goes
back to 1969 when we were, as they say, "young and gay."
With two other friends (one of them Jo's sister), we had set off
for a tour of the southeast, four of us and a suitcase crammed
into my VW bug for the 2,000-mile journey. The rationale for
this madness was to show Jo the "real" America, and our
itinerary read like an AAA Triptik. We had a lot of laughs on
that trip. Like in Williamsburg when a brand new red Chevy
crashed into the car in front of it because the driver, a young
dude who knew a good thing when he saw it, was staring so
intently at Jo (who cut quite a figure with her long red hair and
elegant carriage). I can still see her, wide-eyed in wonderment,

as she tried on flowery hats at Disney World, or awed by the artistry of Preservation Hall's self-taught musicians, or in pensive thought at a Civil War museum in Atlanta. Everything was a wonder to Jo, who was one of the most feeling people I ever knew: for her, life was rich with possibility and ripe for laughter—unless tears were more appropriate. She was generous to a fault with both.

Rose Kushner was a self-proclaimed "professional breast cancer patient." She was also a wife, a mother, a journalist, a volunteer, an activist, and a change agent. Almost single-handedly, Rose won for women the right to a two-step procedure (in which a woman is told the results of her biopsy before any further decisions are made regarding treatment or surgery), and her investigative writing and research undoubtedly led to the end of routine radical mastectomy. Rose was feisty. Stubborn. Difficult at times. Wonderfully difficult. That was how she made things happen, and changed for women around the world their right to participate in decisions regarding their own cancer experiences. There is a story about Rose in her obituary in the Washington Post (January 9, 1990) that bears retelling. While she was a journalist covering the Vietnam War, another columnist said of her, "she has been able to surmount the difficulties of Saigon traffic in an increasingly depressing campaign to find out what the U.S. is doing wrong. Her tentative conclusion is 'everything'." She might well have said the same thing if asked ten years ago what the medical establishment was doing wrong in regard to breast cancer. The thing about Rose, who was 60 when she died, was that having figured that out, she set about to put it right.

The death of people we love, admire, and enjoy—especially when it comes in such untimely a way—is a difficult and sad occasion to bear. We must give ourselves adequate time to grieve and to separate from those good, good people whom we will miss so much. But then, when the time for grieving is past, and we can begin to remember without so much pain, we must take joy from the best that these special human beings have to give the world in our memory of them. That, in many ways, is their living legacy and each of us who was close to them bear the responsibility of remembering.

When I think of Gilda, it is most often as Baba Wawa. The very mention of it cracks me up. Jo lives in my memory as a vision of blue-eyed wonder who quite literally made a smashing impression on everyone who ever saw her. And Rose I see most vividly at a podium or microphone, gravel-voiced and intense as she demanded accountability from an all-too-often arrogant medical audience. She brought them to their knees, then to their feet, and finally to their senses—and for that, we all owe her one.

For these gifts, I am grateful, and bound forever to the joyful memory of these dear friends and very special women.

Experiences In Mothering, Wifing, And Keeping Cool

PRIDE AND PROGENY

"Of all the lunacies earth can boast, the one that must please the devil most, is pride," wrote a 19th century poet named Robert Brough. Samuel Coleridge agreed. "And the devil did grin, for his darling sin, is pride that apes humility." If what they wrote is true, the devil is having a right old time with me lately, laughing himself silly.

I'm sure neither Brough nor Coleridge had mother-pride in mind when they penned their poetry. Nevertheless, it provides an interesting concept for the embarrassing phenomenon which has attacked me lately with alarming frequency and force. In my case, however, "pride goeth before destruction," as promised in the Old Testament. Allow me to set the scene.

My daughter, The Actress, is about to perform in a recital. She and eight other talented teenagers will sing the same song, individually rendered, for their parents, prior to a public appearance. The event takes place in the teacher's studio, a small room in the basement of her house. Unlike a theatre, there is nowhere to hide, no way to pretend the suppressed sobs and snivels came from someone else. The girls are lined up, nervously waiting their turns. I have only to look at them, ingenues all, to feel the lump growing in my throat like a cauliflower captured by a time camera. As the first one gazes into the distance above the heads of her audience and begins the ballad, I enter into Stage I of Losing It. My daughter grits her teeth and rolls her eyes, silently pleading for me to get a grip on myself. To the girl next to her, she whispers, "Oh my God: Look at my mom, and it's not even ME!" By the time it is her turn, I am so far gone that I have bitten my bottom lip bloody. It is all I can do not to let out funereal wails. My husband passes me a clean handkerchief; my tissues have long since disintegrated and shrivelled into pieces—much as I am doing when it's finally over. Other parents shy away from me, wondering if I have recently suffered a great tragedy, uneasy about what to say. I attempt to be lighthearted. "I just can't take it. These kids are so great!" And with that I burst into tears again and have to excuse myself.

Scene change. My son is in line to receive his sixth grade diploma. Like the others, he is full of spit and polish, and seems so grown up that I am suddenly aware of my own years. As the processional begins, I feel the old cauliflower-throat and reach for my tissues. Cherub by cherub they march on stage in the school auditorium. My son, knowing exactly how I will be reacting, scans the audience, and finding my blotched face in the crowd, gives me the I-Caught-You-Grin, which is all I need to really let fly.

The scenes, real and imagined, go on and on, frequently prompted by other people's life events. Weddings, bar mitzvahs, holidays, sitcoms, commercials—in short, any semblance of ceremony and ritual—and I have the devil on my shoulder, having the time of his life. "How you gonna get through your own kids' weddings, huh? What about when they go off to college, how 'bout that? What if they do something wonderful for your 50th birthday, or your 25th anniversary, then what?" he taunts.

The devil is right, of course, but I try not to listen, even though the syndrome seems to get worse with age. (I now weep copious tears over greeting card messages, signed sentimentally during the annual Let's-See-Who-Can-Get-Mom-First-and-Worst Competition.) After all, the devil never had any kids, as far as I know, and neither did Alexander Pope when he wrote, "What the weak head with strongest bias rules, is Pride, the never-failing vice of fools." And moms.

Praise the Lord (and pass the Kleenex).

DRIVING ME CRAZY

I'm not going to make it. I'm simply not going to survive my children's teen years psychologically intact. It's not that they're taking drugs or drinking or in any way messing up their moral characters; it's that they're driving. And pretty well at that. My daughter, who just finished driver's ed with flying colors, is careful, cautious, and courteous behind the wheel. So are most of her friends. It's all the other maniacs I worry about while waiting for them to get home! If the other evening is any anxiety barometer, I have, to borrow from Eugene O'Neill, "a very long day's journey into night." Allow me to share an hour in the life of a waiting-up mother.

11:30 p.m.: An hour before my daughter is due back, I take note of the time and pride myself on my utter calm.

11:45 p.m.: I vow to maintain my calm even into a 15-minute grace period if she should happen to be a little late.

11:55 p.m.: I casually check to see that the skies are still clear and begin a cool inventory of the sorts of things that can detain kids coming out of a movie at the mall. These distractions include such things as stopping in the bathroom, last minute giggles and gossip, forgetting where the car is parked, and losing the car keys.

12:01 a.m.: I shut out all but the front and hall lights and crawl into bed with a book, listening all the while for the sound of sirens.

12:05 a.m.: I realize that I have been reading the same sentence for a full four minutes and still don't understand what it says.

12:07 a.m.: "How long can it take to come home from the mall?" I ask my husband who replies to the rhetorical question with a sleepy shrug.

12:08 a.m.: I get up and look out the front window, willing a particular automobile down the street. I am amazed at how many other cars pass my house at that hour.

12:09 a.m.: I crawl back into bed, staring again at the same sentence in my novel, utterly determined not to be hysterical or foolish.

12:12 a.m.: I get up and put on my best robe for when the policemen arrive.

12:13 a.m.: I pace in front of the window listening for the sound of an approaching vehicle and hope it does not have a red light spinning on top of it when it gets to my house.

12:15 a.m.: I check the movie listings to determine when the last show would have let out, allowing for such contingencies in my calculations as a late start, a faulty projector, and a temporary power failure in the theatre—despite perfectly clear weather.

12:18 a.m.: I make a desperate attempt to calm down, telling myself how utterly stupid I'm being, and more importantly, that I cannot live like this for the next ten years—which is how long it will take for both my kids to be living far enough away that I will never know what time they come home.

12:20 a.m.: The front door opens suddenly to the lyrical sound of "Hi, I'm home!" I manage a smile and a weak, "Have fun?" "Gosh, Mom," my daughter says, "you're so pale! What's wrong?" "Nothing," I reply coolly. "I'm just a little tired. 'Night."

12:23 a.m.: I crawl into bed as butterflies in my stomach give way to a tension headache. "I'm not going to make it," I say to my husband who mutters an understanding "Mmmmmmmmm" and rolls over.

12:28 a.m.: In an attempt to fall asleep, I try variations on a theme of counting sheep, working out in my head just how many weekends there are in ten years. The answer, give or take, makes me blanch.

12:30 a.m.: I consider taking an aspirin but decide instead that reading is a less pathological remedy. This time I understand the words swimming before me as I sink into sleep, rich with relief now that my kids are both safely tucked in.

BONDING

I had just crawled into bed with the *New York Times Book Review*—my reward for surviving a harrowing day of professional and domestic detail—when my daughter burst in on the scene like Sarah Bernhardt.

"I can't believe it!" she wailed. "I didn't get the part!" Her disappointment was as genuine as her shock. After several years of sailing into the lead role in children's community theater, we had both been complacent about the latest try-out. "They want me to be in chorus. Chorus! Are they crazy?"

"That would seem regressive," I offered.

"But if I pull out, they'll think I'm just a snob 'cause I didn't get the part. Besides, it was so much fun last year. Maybe I should do it. Or maybe I should try dinner theater. Oh, I don't know," she cried. "I'm so confused!"

After an hour or so of considered counseling regarding the professionalism of her pending decision, including its moral implications and practical consequences, I realized something more was going on when she flung herself on the bed with great heaving sobs. "I don't have a boyfriend, I'm too skinny, and my friends aren't paying attention to me!"

This apparent string of nonsequiturs made sense once I identified the theme as rejection. My daughter, I realized, was having her first bona fide adolescent crisis.

Suddenly, I remembered her as a baby, so sweet with roly-poly legs flailing around when I changed her diapers. In those harrowing days when child care consumed every ounce of energy I had, I used to imagine how much fun it would be to sit by my daughter's side as she suffered the pangs of puberty. How good I was in my fantasy—a patient and profound soulmate, pillar of wisdom and good advice. It would be such fun to share her agonies!

"You have no idea how much I've looked forward to this," I said after a respectful period of silence during her mourning. The remark stunned her. "Looked forward to what?"

"Sitting by your side while you suffered," I explained, filling in the bits about my fantasies during her infancy.

"You did? Wow!" she said, viewing me with what I think was a certain amount of awe.

"I always imagined it would be such fun, and I'd be so good at it. But you know what?" I offered in solemn confession, "I don't think I'm very good at all, it's not exactly fun, and frankly, I just wanna go to bed. Maybe it's just that your hormones and my hormones are raging in opposite directions just now. Whadaya think?"

"Let's get those hormones in sync!" she said, breaking out in a grin, reminding me how very pretty she is when her eyes twinkle.

All at once, the scene seemed uproariously funny to both of us and we collapsed on the bed, giggling like schoolgirls at a pajama party. It was a good, good moment—even better than any I had dreamed. Then we talked. About guys and values and responsibilities and friendship. I saw that my baby was growing into a beautiful woman—someone I liked and was proud to be connected to.

The next day, she called me at the office, to report on her hormones, and to inquire about mine. "Holding steady," I said, "But can you believe it? That story I wrote was rejected. I'm behind on a deadline, and God, I feel fat!"

"You know," she said in tones of false mockery, "I always thought it would be so much fun to counsel my mother in a crisis. But you know what? It's not really fun. So shape up, kid!"

"You got it," I said. "See ya later."

"Love you."

"Love you too."

I smiled at the ritual of farewell which has been in place since she first talked. The bonds were strong then too. But this is different. This time, the heartstrings of womanhood are part of the glue binding us to one another. And no fantasy in the world can compete with that.

If you don't believe me, just ask my daughter, The Actress. Because when it comes to bonding, all the Bernhardts and Barrymores in the world couldn't hold a candle to her performance. It's a definite Oscar.

Parenting: Part II

"Just you wait," everyone said. "It gets so much more complicated!"

It seemed at the time like all the other inane and off-the-cuff remarks that people make mindlessly to new parents. Like "Don't wish the time away. They grow up before you know it!" Or "Enjoy it! You won't remember what they were like at this stage."

I found these comments irritating and silly in the days when I would have given anything to crawl into bed for more than four hours at a time, or to shave my legs in peace. In their own way these comments were as punishing as the unsolicited judgments that others felt entitled to make about everything from pacifiers to diaper rash.

But they were right. It is hard to remember my gangly, pubescent offspring as peach-complexioned cherubs. They have suddenly grown up before my unseeing eyes (while I haven't aged a bit, of course). Most of all, it does get much more complicated.

In retrospect, life was easy before the days of orthodonture, music lessons, academic competition, and first dates. In the good old days, all you had to worry about was whether the diaper bag was properly packed and the sitter was on time. Once convinced that the person to whom you had entrusted your child was not a closet pervert, you could go off happily, knowing that your containable, commandable child would be safe. Even overnight respites were possible, with telephone check-ins assuring that your house had not burnt down, been burgled, or added to the number of sudden infant deaths.

Gone are the days when shoving peas up their noses was probably the worst that could happen. Today's terrors are much bigger. It isn't just whether the nuclear holocaust will happen while we're out of town, or whether the plagues of our day will be visited on our homes.

Equally worrying is the fear that our children will just once, at exactly the wrong moment, forget to be wise; that despite what we so carefully have taught them, they will follow instead of lead, join in when they should have held out, be influenced by "other kids." Suddenly, in the midst of night terrors, our children—sweet toddlers only yesterday—seem strangers in a hostile and seductive world.

In these anxious moments, it's hard to remember that in our day, to someone else's mother, we were the other kid helping to fuel the fantasies of disaster. It was our judgment called into question, our choices untrusted. But somehow, we survived, and grew wise enough to be parents in spite of ourselves. It is this that we must remember calmly in moments of panic when we fear for our children.

Things may not be quite as they were in those days. Times change, to be sure; but being a parent doesn't. It's just that, like everyone said, it gets more complicated.

RAISING TEENAGERS IN AFFLUENT AMERICA

L ately I've been reflecting on how we raise teenagers in A-
merica's affluent suburbs. I can't say I like what I see. But
the image that assaults me most glaringly in the mirror of my
mind's eye is of me as a parent, the so-called responsible adult
in the relationship.

But are we? After all, parents—in the name of boys-will-be-
boys—allow toddlers to fling objects at each other just because
their overalls have zippers. Similarly, we participate in the
collective con of teenage atrocities. In fact, we create the
norms. We have allowed for a standard which dictates that by
age twelve a personal telephone is sheer necessity. We roll our
eyes but nevertheless our daughters sashay around in designer
blue jeans with matching T-shirts made to look like last year's
faded beach towels. God forbid we should say "No!" to our
kids or deprive them the pleasures of their peers. Meanwhile,
the ceiling of indulgence, like inflation, keeps rising.

Nor is it just material indulgence that worries me. Even more
troubling is how excessively self-centered these kids can be. In
my day, being part of a family meant being involved in a small
community. Everyone was expected to contribute, to compromise, to chip in. Nowadays, many kids seem more like high-
class boarders, checking in to eat and get the laundry done,
while beating a path between TV and refrigerator.

I tried explaining this to my fourteen-year-old daughter after
her birthday party (which of course involved putt-putt, pizza,
and a slumber party. Anything less would have seemed tacky,
if not boring, by local standards).

She groaned, "Oh, Mom, don't take a spazz," after I tried
to explain why I was upset when five teenagers had attempted
to curl up in one living room chair simultaneously.

"I have standards," I pouted. "There are rules. We just redecorated." But what I thought was, why do I feel so guilty?

"None of the other mothers get so mad," my daughter said accusingly. And then the illumination occurred. None of us, I suddenly realized, is setting any codes of conduct for this energized population! Oh, we've taught our kids to say "please" and "thank you" and not to pick their noses in public. But it seems that nobody is holding these youngsters accountable for respecting the physical or psychological space of others. The values of courtesy and compromise have slipped silently out of our repertoire of expectation. Rather, by the sin of commission, I feel guilty for creeping downstairs at 2:00 a.m. to ask that the decibel level be lowered enough so that others can sleep. When I am irritable because no one has cleared the ice cream, I appear aberrant. My daughter gives me "The Look" when I suggest that running around like a banshee is an outdoor activity, and I slink away feeling decidedly middle-aged because of my limited tolerance.

But wait, says a voice of reason from within. You're the grown-up. It's okay to expect a little thoughtfulness. Maybe, just maybe, these kids are getting away with too much.

Then slowly, out of a sense of legitimacy, comes renewed vigor and self-respect. I explain to my daughter in no uncertain terms what my limitations are and what constitutes an infraction. Consequences are articulated clearly (knowing that the hard part will be implementing them the first time). Amazingly, my teenager reacts with support and relief once parameters are set. "Isn't it great," she says, "when you think you've done something wrong and then you find out you haven't?" I overhear her telling a friend "where my mom is coming from" and I let her finish before calling her a second time to help with dinner. I know she'll appear momentarily because she won't want to suffer telephone restriction. Besides, after the third beckoning, she understands that we are moving to rural America. And I get to pick where, 'cause I'm the grown-up.

THE CASE OF THE
MERCHANDISE MANIAC

We thought absolutely nothing of it when the realtor rang up to see when he could appraise the house we were selling. My husband responded to him exactly as he had to the insurance salesman who purportedly was responding to a bounceback card. "Sorry, there must be some mistake."

When the computer magazines started showing up, however, we thought perhaps the matter needed looking into. "Anyone around here know about this?" we asked at dinner one night. My daughter responded innocently enough in the negative, but I noticed that my son suddenly developed an appetite remarkable even for a growing ten-year-old.

Several days later, a notice arrived in the mail thanking us for our order of $50 worth of tulip bulbs which we could look forward to receiving in time for spring planting. This was followed by a request for correction in our credit card number from an amiable company in California so that the $231 toy order could be shipped.

I was beginning to get the picture.

Our son, who has a penchant for hoarding junk mail, "just to play office," was summoned.

"What do you know about this?" we demanded.

"Nothing!" he proclaimed, a downward glance darting between me and my husband.

"Nothing?"

"I was just playing. I didn't mean to mail it."

"You call that toy company and tell them what you did!" I screeched like a fishwife.

No sooner had we sorted that out when the blood pressure cuff arrived with exquisite efficiency from a merchandising center in Iowa. It was just in time: my blood pressure had reached stroke proportions and now, when I opened my mouth to shriek, nothing came out but a hoarse whisper. "We'll all go to jail for mail fraud," I gasped.

"Don't be silly," said my rational husband. "We'll just return it, cancel our credit card, and give him a sound beating." Having taken care of the first and second items on the agenda, we chastised our son roundly, sending him off to bed with no supper and a week's worth of restrictions which allowed for little more than breathing. He promised to cease and desist immediately. The matter appeared to be settled.

Until the security heat lamps showed up. "It's pipeline," my husband said as I applied a cold compress to my forehead.

"Do you realize how much junk mail has prepaid postage on it?" I asked, shivering. "We could be in 'pipeline' from now till our case goes to court!"

The following day I stayed home from work with a killer headache. I realized what a stroke of luck this was when I saw the UPS truck pull up. Before the driver could off-load the two file cabinets, I bounded out of the house, screaming "No! No! There's been a mistake!"

"This is your address?" she asked.

"Yes, but...."

"My, you do a lot of catalog shopping, don't you?"

I explained that my son was the compulsive consumer.

"How entrepreneurial!" she exclaimed. "My son would never have thought of it."

"One woman's entrepreneur is another woman's aggravation," I sighed.

"Don't worry, dear. I'll send it all back if it's addressed to him." Never has a stranger felt so much like a best friend. Maybe we have her to thank for the fact that no packages have shown up on the doorstep lately. Now I lie awake at night wishing she could help us convince Sears that we really don't owe them $148.50 for the cabinets we returned.

But things are gradually returning to normal, and I've begun to face each day with a diminishing fear of what it will bring—literally. Of course, I'm never complacent. I know that every delivery truck is a potential enemy when you live with a merchandise maniac. Just to be cautious, I shred the junk mail every day now, and make sure that credit cards are never left lying around. The system is foolproof.

That's why I'm absolutely sure the investment broker made a random error when he called to change the appointment he says we set. I know for a fact that it wasn't my son who called the lawn service last Saturday. He spent the day thumbing through catalogs.

Funny, but for some unknown reason, they seem to be inundating our mailbox these days.

HAIL BRITTANIA: THE PLEASURES AND PITFALLS OF MARRYING A BRIT

S eventeen years ago, it annoyed me enormously when a re-
porter friend of ours announced in *The London Times* that
my husband was leaving his post in the British Treasury because of his American fiancee. To this day I bristle at the
suggestion that I came to know England because of him. The
fact is, having worked in London in the 1960's, I was an
Anglophile long before we met. To this day, I have seen more
of the UK than my British-born spouse—granted, at the super-
ficial level of a tourist with an appallingly limited knowledge
of English history.

Nevertheless, I still have difficulty in determining whether
some of my husband's habits are part of the national character,
or uniquely his own. Certainly his sense of honour (or, as we
Americans say, honor) suggests something noble beyond
individual attribute. It was one of the first traits that drew me
to him—more out of curiosity than admiration, I must admit.
Here was a man who, by the third date, hadn't made a move.
My ego was sufficiently intact to believe it was his problem, but
with the conditioning of an American woman, the situation
certainly suggested pathology. In the nick of time, he convinced me otherwise.

This same code of honour nearly got me in trouble in other
ways. Shortly after we became engaged we took a train journey. On the return to London, the conductor neglected to
collect our tickets. Feeling as though I had just won at Ascot,
I suggested we turn them in for a rebate, as any full-blooded
American would have done. My husband-to-be was horrified,
however, that I would even contemplate cheating British Rail.
The episode nearly cost me my engagement ring.

Honour may be one thing, but humour is quite another. Can it really be that all British men are so . . . I grope for the word . . . puerile? I mean, here is a man who actually thinks Benny Hill is funny; a man who once convulsed himself with mirth at the spontaneous suggestion that Dr. Christian Barnard was really "a heartless fellow." Even our children cringe now when they see their father chortling quietly to himself as he listens to John Cleese tapes.

Personal habits are another thing I wonder about. Do all Englishmen, for example, take a glass of water to bed with them with religious regularity, knocking it over in the middle of the night with absolute predictability at least twice a month? And do they tuck a handkerchief under their pillows at night, forgetting always to remove it in the morning to the horror of wives and hotel chambermaids? (And in the age of Kleenex, who needs to save it in the first place?)

One learns to live with this sort of thing in the end. But there are other idiosyncracies far more threatening to the Anglo-American marriage. Take formality. Anglos have it; Americans don't. In the early days of our married life, my husband (who came to America as a diplomat) positively cringed whenever I suggested that our guests help themselves to another drink. God forbid I took paper plates on a picnic! Potluck dinners were definitely out. Consequently, our social life dropped off to nearly nil; everyone lived in mortal fear of having to reciprocate.

We've worked through the entertainment crises over the years, but other challenges remain. We still argue over whether it's hot enough to turn on the air conditioner (my husband is the only human being I know who thinks of Panama as temperate), what to pack for holiday ("But, dear, you simply won't be able to get through the whole of Proust in two weeks. Besides, do you really need to take it all in hardback?"), and how many hand-me-downs can reasonably be carried transatlantic on one trip.

But I wouldn't trade it for the world, and neither would my children, who have grown up with Mr. Men, Beatrix Potter,

Arthur Rackham, Marks & Spencer, Mothercare, and Queen Mum. These biculture kids know what bacon and bangers are all about. They were weaned on tea and scones, followed by trifle and Queen's pudding, and they can tuck into a joint with Yorkshire pud. They are in love with Big Ben, Madame Toussaud, and the West End. And, as my daughter once said with enormous pride when she was five years old, they speak two languages: English and American.

As for me, I no longer "get my knickers in a twist" over the little things, and I don't mind anymore "having the mickey taken out." After all, no American husband I know calls his wife "Darling," unless he's sending a greeting card. Most of them forget their anniversaries, and few remember to tell their wives on each birthday that they look "absolutely smashing."

More importantly, after 18 years, I value Britain's virtues, tolerate its foibles, and cherish new traditions built on the best that both sides of the Atlantic have to offer. For, to borrow from Alice Duer Miller's splendid "White Cliffs,"

"I am American bred,
I have seen much to hate here—much to forgive,
But in a world (without Englishmen),
I do not wish to live."

GREETINGS FROM THE CONTROL ROOM

"Happy Birthday to the man who has everything," the card said, "and never throws any of it away." Perfect, I thought, grabbing it off the shelf, as countless other wives must have done. After all, Hallmark doesn't exactly specialize in one-of-a-kind greetings.

The revelation that other women struggle with conjugal chaos was momentarily reassuring. Perhaps the world harbors a secret society of straighteners—people like myself who have a compulsion for order, matched with maniacs who thrive on disarray. The tricky bit in living with people driven to saving and strewing is to keep cool in the face of clutter, surreptitiously creating little centers of chaos control to project the illusion of a system, while the "pack rat" partner—who can only function with the aid of a seeing eye dog—never notices that anything is askew.

It took me years to work this out; ironically, I have my husband to thank. At the risk of sounding like Henny Youngman—who, for those too young to know, made a fortune on the one-liner, "Take my wife . . . please!"—my husband's penchant for disorder approaches fine art. Here is a man whose wallet has flown solo to Detroit and back (both he and the wallet having originated in London), who on waking in the morning cannot find his pants (which I assure him came home on him the night before), whose perpetual refrain is "Anyone seen my glasses?" (Read also checkbook/keys/briefcase.) This is the charmer who was dubbed "Mr. Weekender" by my daughter at the age of four, because he is always going to find it, fix it, or finish it during those precious two days.

Unfortunately, things have gone from bad to worse, which I only realized during a recent phone conversation with his secretary, who had called to see if I could find his calendar.

"I can't take it anymore," I wailed. "You give the man a drawer, he'll stuff it. Give him a table, he'll cover it. Give him a room, he'll fill it!"

"I know," she commiserated. "He now takes up two offices and he's spilling over into a third."

At that point, I paused for a silent moment of prayer—that I should die first. If not, I will simply burn every single record, file, paper, and folder I can put my hands on, and go into my Butterfly McQueen act with the lawyers: "But I don't know nothin' 'bout all these legal affairs, Sir!"

Not long ago, I clipped an article by a clutter-control expert and laid it lovingly on my husband's pillow. I had underscored the bit that said "If you haven't read it, smelled it, touched it, or kissed it in the last five years, you don't need it," (or words to that effect). He chuckled and tossed it onto the pile of papers on his bedside table, some of which date back to 1978.

I knew then that I had to take control of the situation, and that is when I began making piles out of pandemonium. I have since honed the skill, throwing out any drugstore receipts, catalogs, or advertisements which predate our marriage. I don't bat an eye as my husband weaves through the stacks I've created, mumbling about getting to it at the weekend. I routinely ask, as we depart for anywhere, "Have you got your glasses, wallet, checkbook, keys?"

Some people may see this as a copout, but for me it's a major achievement. My husband is coming along nicely too. This year, after reading his birthday cards, he actually let me throw out the envelopes. From where I sit, which is smack in the middle of mission control, that's real progress.

MARRY MR. FIXIT IF YOU CAN

"**F**or all the jobs your husband never gets around to, call Jim," the ad read. Oh, man of my dreams! I thought as I clipped the tiny square box from the newspaper with all the fervor of a computer dating addict. Clever Jim. A marketing genius, he had hit the nail right on the head (so to speak), identifying his target audience as those of us married to well-intentioned and reasonably handy men who seem to be forever otherwise engaged.

My own husband is a pretty talented guy. He can deal with leaky faucets, faulty wires, stubborn appliances, and a wide array of other household annoyances. He's wonderful in the garden and marginal in the garage. His resourcefulness knows no bounds: he has been known to open wine bottles with a fork when all else fails.

Partial exhibits of my husband's talents are visible in every corner of the house and yard. The flower beds around the trees in the front garden are a showcase; unfortunately, those in the back haven't quite been planted yet because to do so would require transporting the mound of earth deposited on our driveway some months ago—which now needs to be weeded in order to serve its purpose. My daughter's bedroom will look wonderful with its new color scheme of gray and white once the painting is finished, so I try not to dwell on the 13 years she went without a second coat of pink waiting for the first to dry properly. I'm sure that before winter comes again we'll be able to get the car into the garage. It's just a simple matter of getting a few hooks up on the wall to organize the ladders, bikes, roof rack, garden supplies, and tools.

First, however, there is the matter of filing last year's income tax returns and submitting the medical insurance reimbursements. These tasks should be easier next year once the filing system my husband designed shortly after we were married in 1972 is set up. In the course of sorting through the papers to be filed, we're hoping that our Last Will and a few other documents will surface in the shuffle of paper. My husband, like Dickens' Mr. McCawber, assures me that they are "bound to turn up."

I'm sure he's right, and that our situation isn't unique. After all, everyone needs a wife, and every wife needs a Jim. Which leads me to wonder only one thing: Who does Jim's wife call when her toilet overflows? Not that Jim won't get around to it one of these days; but in the meantime, I know just how she feels.

THERE'S A REASON WHY THEY CALL IT WORK

MANAGING THE MANAGERS

N oel Coward was once asked what he said to actors back-
stage after a poor performance of one of his plays. "I
always say the same thing," he replied. "My, what a remarkable performance!"

That anecdote puts me in mind of a lot of people I know who
aren't writing brilliant plays, but who are playing brilliantly.
The game is called Office Politics, and when it comes to tact,
Coward had nothing up on the average middle manager whose
creative bent is often applied to stroking the guy with the gold
plated key to the executive washroom.

This middle man, as it turns out, is often a woman: in the
classic case study, she is in her early thirties; has worked her
way up to the middle ranks from a secretarial position; probably has taught her boss most of what he knows; and statistically
speaking, hasn't a hope in hell of getting much higher on the
corporate ladder. She endears herself, wittingly or otherwise,
to the boss by taking on the role of the office wife-mother. He
may not agree with her judgments (she rarely gets to make
decisions), but they certainly help to shape his own. He is
decidedly bent out of shape when she is not around to bounce
an idea off, and his casual "Whadaya think?" is frequently a
thinly veiled plea for help. She subtly plants the seeds of
strategy, covers the contingencies, and ensures that any faux
pas is forgiven, all the while organizing and prioritizing from
a quasi-privileged if invisible vantage point.

This convenient, if somewhat symbiotic, arrangement may
ensue for years. But invariably, a moment of truth challenges
the status quo, altering irrevocably the balance of power on an
ethical if not a practical plane. For many women this moment
can be cataclysmic, a sunburst of sensitivity to the realities of

workplace dynamics. For others less prone to spiritual experience, the effect is powerful nonetheless. Consider the following true scenario reported by a friend seasoned in the ways of work life.

"You want to WHAT?"
"I want to promote him."
"But he's utterly incompetent!"
"I know. He's driving me crazy. That's why I want to promote him. Gotta get him outa here."

The episode proved to be a turning point for my friend. She remembers it clearly as a watershed event in her decision to "go independent" as a free-lance consultant. "I just couldn't go along with the institutionalized rewarding of incompetence and ignoring or punishment of competence. It just seemed to put things in perspective for me. Here I was dealing with everything from conflict resolution to contract management and getting nowhere, and this guy who couldn't function was moving right on up the ladder, safety net intact."

But my friend's rite of passage wasn't completed until her boss said his final farewell. "It's just as well," he grinned, putting his arm around her shoulder. "Would have been pretty hard to promote someone as attractive as you without people starting to talk!"

My friend was speechless. But I'll bet I know what Noel Coward would have said. What a remarkable performance, indeed.

THE CULTURE OF CORPORATE
CONSULTING

Jennifer is an experienced professional, savvy in the ways of the workplace. Technically competent and a good manager, she prides herself on her resourceful approach to career change. Still, she paid a lot of dues before psyching out what was happening when she tried to transition from a public interest organization to a well-respected business firm. Frequently called in to mop up, map out, or manage temporarily, she watched the carrots of long-term opportunity being dangled before her dissipate one by one. "I began to feel like a down comforter," she recalls. "All filler and fluff!" Repeated assurances that the company would hire her as soon as they could never materialized. The response to her follow-up calls became a cool "Don't-call-us; we'll-call-you"—which the company never hesitated to do when they needed a quick fix.

Helen worked for the same company for nearly ten years. Shunted from project to project as deemed necessary by the corporate execs, she consistently worked 60-hour weeks in order to do her job and develop proposals for new business—the profit-making equivalent of "publish or perish." Then she made the mistake of needing surgery. When she returned to the office several weeks later, she found herself replaced, and her office moved to smaller quarters. She received a clear message that unless she could generate new revenue, she might no longer have a role in the organization.

Marie had been made Vice President in the same firm after nearly a decade of service because of the business she brought in. A mid-fifties professional, she and her husband had agreed to a commuter marriage when he was transferred because of her dedication to her job. Eighteen months later, a major contract she directed was lost to a competitor. At an officer's meeting shortly afterwards, Marie was advised that she should be writing herself into an upcoming proposal as an administrator (a junior position)—the implication being that her continued tenure resided in that option.

These women all work for the same firm, which has a solid history, a portfolio worth millions of dollars, and an avowed pride in its philosophy of an ethical and caring work environment.

That all of the people involved are women may be significant. It is, after all, well known that the world of work is inundated with trousered incompetence. I suspect, though, that this scenario says more about the corporate culture of consulting than about gender issues in the workplace. The examples of Jennifer, Helen, and Marie are but a microcosm of life in the fast track of business and bucks.

The issue of financial viability notwithstanding, surely there is a better way. Somewhere between this atmosphere and the sloth of perennial parasites often characterized by civil servants immune from dismissal, there must be a model for business firms that allows for a humane and moral workplace. Standing back from the business production line, which is really only a high class version of any factory, might it not be possible to re-evaluate the method of marketplace competition? Wouldn't it, in the end, be more profitable to establish a means of retaining competent, creative, and dedicated staff?

Perhaps further exploration of this radical concept is worth a few days of a consultant's time. No doubt a Jennifer, Helen, or Marie could put her shoulder to the task if asked. Of course, such a perspective would mean taking risks, not to mention admitting the readiness to innovate.

So, on second thought, don't call them. They'll call you—just as soon as they can figure out how to make themselves billable and business firms accountable.

It's a call that might take some time coming.

OUT OF THE MOUTHS OF
BABES . . . AND BOYS

I n the field of communication, which happens to be what I studied in graduate school, you can get a thesis under your belt in some nifty ways. If you're interested in such things as "source credibility" and "gender communication" (which I am), you can actually do your research while working the room at a cocktail party—or while just plain working. The field is wide open, especially to women, who seem to be the only ones subject to wonder why, for example, no one ever listens to them, or how it is that they are subject to such constant interruption by the various men in their lives.

You save a lot of time in the initial literature review because, relative to the topics that turn men on—like "meta level paradigms" and "linear models of interpersonal communication"—precious little in the stacks explains why men are rude, women are passive, and "nine out of ten (male) doctors recommend Advil." However, the literature that can be found is pretty interesting stuff. Studies show, for instance, that when husbands accompany their pregnant wives to the obstetrician, the physician stops talking to the woman and addresses himself solely to the father-to-be. Similarly, when a woman in a group raises a question, the answer is almost always directed at the male(s) present. It has been demonstrated repeatedly that men interrupt women with alarming frequency, and that males have an uncontrollable penchant for interpreting what they think the little woman was trying to say. If you don't believe this, pay close attention to the dynamics of the conversation the next time you are out for dinner.

I thought about this recently at a meeting I was participating in having to do with the health care decisions that women in developing countries make. Some years ago, I had suggested that this same "expert" group needed to pay closer attention to what in communication jargon is called "social support systems": friends, family, networks. My suggestion went unheeded. Then one day not very long ago, at a similar forum, a male colleague of mine got up and said with professorial authority, "I think we need to be looking at social influences at the community level," and, hey presto, it's been a part of the paradigm ever since. This time, as I pleaded the importance of interpersonal communication at the household level to shed light on decision making and health behaviors (e.g., does her husband let her out of the house to go to the clinic if it means he has to wait for dinner?), I saw the same glazed look cross the eyes of my worthy comrades. There she goes again, they were no doubt thinking, off on another of her liberal-feminist-Marxist-out-in-left-field tangents. But mark my words. One of these days, one of these jocks is going to jump up and take the position that it's high time we started looking at household communication structures and Hosanna! We will start looking at household communication structures. That, my friends, is source credibility.

Which is why male actors in white lab coats sell aspirin. And why male, middle-aged MD's (the sacred 3M's) have not been made to feel ridiculous when they tell us about childbirth. ("You don't have to have a brain tumor to be a neurosurgeon!" An argument just about as spurious as this one: "If God meant you to fly, you would have been born with wings.") And why men feel entitled to interrupt, interpret, and trivialize a sizable portion of what represents our own sound thinking on a given issue.

At the meeting I attended, one of the men used an expression so extraordinary that I wrote it down. "Truthful reporting made use of," is what he said. I don't remember the exact context but essentially it had to do with what (women) subjects tell (men) researchers about their daily lives. I don't think he had any idea of what he was actually revealing, and no woman in the room was going to interpret for him—least of all in public (not out of passivity, mind you, just politeness). But more than a few of us were jolted by the unintended honesty of his remark; for here, once again, was the male authority, only too ready to take from woman's reality what was useful for his own purpose and his own progress, while she remained silent and invisible.

There is historical precedent for this behavior, and it has to do with economics. Simply put, you show me some research dollars and I'll show you a man with a sudden new interest in women's perception of a problem. But that is perhaps a separate issue, another essay.

The point of this piece is quite simple and has nothing to do really with whether or not you are interested in research and communication theory. It only has to do with whether you'd like to finish a sentence at the dinner table, or have your point of view validated, or your question answered.

That, for many, would be sheer luxury. Ask any woman. You won't find a more credible source.

Star Wars

The young financial manager was the first to go. Bright, energetic, a quick thinker, he had offered a variety of innovations to technocrats who purportedly wanted to enhance the fiscal management of a rapidly growing firm. With all the spirit of a young professional out to prove himself, and all the promise of a rising star, he brought to bear a vision of improved systems based on sound understanding of budget and programs. It didn't take him long to realize, however, that with every new idea there was increased resistance from one executive director or another. At the end, in a pathetically contrived scene that revealed the desperation of one director, he was arbitrarily dismissed.

Soon after, a dynamic young woman was hired for a year, the future of her position contingent on her success. Her mandate? Develop new business. She undertook this task with the vigor of an athlete, using her wits, her professional wisdom, her past contacts, and a good deal of humor. By a stroke of near genius, she identified an opportunity completely overlooked by the competition, and with no organizational resources to support her, set about operationalizing an idea. When she had put things in place, her boss suddenly assigned her to administrative details while he and his boss took off to meet with the contacts she had nurtured. This sort of thing happened once too often to seem inadvertent, and before the end of her "probationary" year, she resigned.

While all of this was going on, another colleague who had been active and articulate in several management retreats found herself increasingly marginalized in discussions of company policy and planning. Her omission on a number of task forces and committees was noticed by several coworkers, who had complimented her astute analysis of problems within the organization's structure and human resource development.

Each of these professionals, and several more like them, seduced by company standards into an Overqualified-Under-employed Syndrome, had committed the unspoken cardinal sin. They had challenged, and therefore threatened, the power brokers with new ways of thinking.

In this case, as it happens, the power brokers, who were still young men, had started their careers with the company in question. Working their way up from clerks and Boys Friday, they had each, under the same mentor, risen like meteors and were now in full if not comfortable command of a visible company with an impressive array of clients and a ''book'' of millions of dollars. But mentoring for others was not in their current portfolio. Managing (some would say controlling) people and programs was, and they prided themselves on their native ability to ''respond to the client.'' This responsiveness often seemed to others (like the financial manager, the development expert, and the management analyst) to leave the company floating in somewhat undirected fashion, like a giant spaceship adrift in a boundless universe. Whenever anyone tried to suggest a little mission control, or a new way of shooting for the stars, the CEO and his vice presidents would say, ''That's how we've always done it. Besides, we're flexible. That's what makes us special.''

The curious thing about their position was that, to some people, it seemed that the company wasn't flexible at all. At least internally, a rigid course had been set that did not allow for the launching of new talent. To those at the helm, the galaxy in which they were floating just wasn't big enough for more than a few shining quasars—which is what they fancied themselves to be. No matter what they said (which was usually the ''right'' thing), it did not go unnoticed that with each new ray of light across the horizon, the power brokers closed their eyes and would not allow them to be pried open—even with the promise of something spectacular to consider. Not ready to give up their piece of turf and failing to realize that within the vast universe of possibility there is room for each and every one of us, they foolishly allow the twinklers of talent to escape into the night, where one day they may well form their own constellations. Ironically, this potential does not seem nearly as threatening as inviting these "aliens" aboard, but perhaps that is not so surprising after all.

No doubt it is rather difficult to "see the light" at the very same time that one is hurtling into a big black hole, ultimately to be sucked into oblivion by the force of Self.

THE HALF-GENERATION GAP

In many respects, they are very much alike: Well-educated, talented, competent, intelligent, reliable. They seem to have every reason to complement each other in the workplace. Why then are they in conflict?

Paula is 46 years old. She graduated from a respectable midwestern university, taught, married, had two children, then returned to the world of work outside the home as an arts administrator. She is also a painter, an avocation she began to honor only recently. She has a sense of reality and a set of priorities shared and respected by the majority of her contemporaries. Paula knows a lot of things and is the equivalent of street-smart because of her life's experience.

Janice is "thirtysomething" and still on the fast track. After graduating with an art history degree from a reputable northeast college, she has come to work at the gallery which Paula manages. Having worked a stint in a Madison Avenue gallery in New York City, she is a very sophisticated, savvy young woman, smart, and full of energy. Still in her ascendancy, Janice feels the world is hers to conquer and that she isn't about to miss anything it has to offer. She is an aspiring young professional; the rest, she says, will come later.

In ways that neither one of them can articulate, each woman has a way of grating on the other. Paula resents Janice's self-assuredness, not in itself, but for the way it contributes to her slightly haughty nature. She can be pushy, almost untrustworthy. Janice feels vaguely threatened by Paula's self-possessed and quiet demeanor, never knowing exactly how to read her and unable to relate to her seeming lack of ambition.

Why are these two women—both competent professionals—uneasy with each other, and in some fundamental way, unreconciled?

Perhaps the problem, only exacerbated by gender, is really

one of age. The thirties, after all, are a time of passion, energy, excitement, possibility. A time when nothing is to be missed, and our own potential tells us we can do it all (if we hurry). In our forties—when we have mellowed out, examined our lives in a way that asks what is real, "lost a few" and been hurt, sometimes in watershed ways—things change. We begin to take a more cosmic, holistic, organic view of our lives and our environment. It becomes easier, and more urgent, to tell the truth about our own foibles, our organizational weaknesses. What we want out of life, as we begin the descent, is not power and prestige, but beauty and space; intimacy and simplicity. We no longer need to apologize, or mask what we know; and we don't much care for games any longer. We have earned the right to be a little "laid back" even as we stand up to peers and painful situations. That is a posture difficult to adopt, or to understand, until one can own the experience of getting there. It is also a position easy to resent, because in some disarming way it is enviable.

Paula is uncomfortable with Janice's aggressive profession-alism and her career aspirations because she sees in these traits a threat to her own equilibrium—the balance she has worked so long and hard to achieve in her own life. Janice feels an uneasiness she can't explain in Paula's calm and easy ability to make choices, articulate options, offer solutions, analyze situations. Somewhere deep inside of her, below conscious but above subliminal, she senses in Paula a woman truly to be admired, emulated even, if only she were ready.

One day, not so very long ago, Paula was thirtysomething too, and she tries now to remember those times. And one day in the not too distant future, Janice will reach her forties as well. It is a decade, a passage to which she cannot yet relate. But perhaps when she gets there, she will remember Paula and understand her a little more fully with the empathy that comes of maturity.

Maybe there will even be a Janice in her own life. If so, it will be nice for her to think about Paula, and how she might have handled things in that even, calm way she had back in the days when they were office, if not soul, mates.

ROSIE THE RIVETER REVISITED

R osie the Riveter is alive and well, I'm sorry to report. Rosie, you will recall, was the prototype of wartime women who worked in the factories while the men were in the trenches. Depicted in a now classic film, Rosie, having kept the war effort going (and having discovered independence and income in the process), was relegated to the kitchen again once Johnny came marching home. After all, having done his duty to God and country (and being, of course, the breadwinner), the job went to Johnny. Forty-plus years postwar, Rosie is no longer in the factory. She is in America's offices, schools, hospitals, and businesses. She is in the small towns and in the big cities. She is you and me. She is my friend Beth who just learned, figuratively speaking, that after four years in the factory, Johnny is marching home again.

Beth has been managing a multimillion dollar worldwide project and was promoted within her first year of employment to assistant director because, in the words of one vice president, she was "the only thing keeping this project glued together." While she dealt with daily operations, budget decisions, numerous subcontractors, various technical issues, and a still unsettled staff, the project director and other assorted males were "in the field" conferencing, cajoling clients, and cutting deals. After about two years, things started to settle down. People began to notice the project and even to hold it up as a model for others. About that time, the boys started crawling out of the trenches to claim victory. Beth noticed that her portfolio wasn't as full as it had once been, but she took advantage of that opportunity to develop new business and to publish articles about the project. She continued to receive excellent annual reviews with appropriate remuneration. When it came time to renew the contract two years later, Beth was confident that she would be rebid as assistant director.

The director told her the reason that she would not be was that while she had "made a real contribution," she had several times expressed an interest in moving from management to the more technical side of things. They were certain, he said, that something "could be worked out," but in the meantime, the bright new kid on the block (of the male variety, of course) would be bid in her position.

It didn't help, of course, that Beth was a card-carrying member of Uppity Women United—that group of women deemed "strident" and "bitchy" when they exhibit the same strategies and decision making techniques of their "competent" male counterparts. Nor was it in her favor (despite the praise of several colleagues) that on more than one occasion she had committed the cardinal sin of innovation and the questioning of male authority. Clearly, it was time for Rosie to beat a retreat.

There are many ways to violate and abuse women without physical force, and of these, none is more painful to bear than the devaluation, trivialization, and marginalization of women's work.

There are also ways to put an end to this acting out of violence against women, which amounts, after all, to nothing more than men's quasi-public acts of masturbation.

Of all these things, none is more effective than reclaiming the power of excellence. That is why Beth, and women like her everywhere, are "going independent"—starting their own businesses and companies, and in record numbers, succeeding in giving the boys a run for their money.

Of course, a little bit of rage and a lot of humor never hurt either. As one successful consultant put it to Beth recently, "Get into a warrior mode. Imagine yourself a Sherman tank mowing them down on the battlefield and fight back. It sure beats guilt and self-deprecation!" My own contribution was only slightly less assertive. I suggested that we all run out and have our third fingers cast in bronze, with the mold placed prominently on our desks in the event of enemy attack, and lovingly inscribed "Here's lookin' at you, Rosie!"

MOTHERS AND MANAGERS: WORKING IT OUT

This may come as a surprise, but back in the seventies when I was having my kids, neither the biological clock nor maternity leave were very prominent topics for young moms. They were there, of course, but not as the burning issues (along with day care) that they are now. Having children within a few years of marriage was still a given, and along with that came the "I'll just take a few years out" fantasy. Anything else was still viewed deep down as marital heresy, although lots of people, including the moms, became adept at pretending otherwise. A lot of us made mistakes under that whip of conventional wisdom about when we had children and how they influenced our work lives, but that is another story.

A few years later, the two issues became ripe for picking. Although they were no longer "my" issues (I'd had my two children and was back at work), I prided myself on being a vocal and vehement sister in support of working moms, with all of its ramifications. I remember going blue in the face when I heard a woman manager being interviewed on radio about how unproductive women were when they returned from maternity leave. "Working mother," she believed, was an oxymoron. Goaded by the interviewer, she divulged her belief that women who had new babies were unreliable, less than productive, and—let's face it—always put the baby's needs first. I still see stars when anyone, particularly another woman, pulls that number.

But I have a confession to make: My womanist ideology is being put to the test by workplace reality. My friend and colleague, you see, just had a baby.

Lynn was a late primipara—42 at the birth of this first baby, born six weeks early following a set of worrisome complications. This prenatal reality meant that Lynn had to cut back to part time work, which was not in the original plan. Her maternity leave clearly commenced before we had anticipated. This obviously threw us off balance, but we compensated nicely, everyone chipping in to take a piece of her workload. Happily she and the baby are doing fine now, and Lynn will return to work next month. Part time. Assuming she can get good child care. Just when a major set of documents and a humongous report are due. Tensions are high in the office, and I can understand why. As a manager, I sympathize with the people I supervise who are on the road to burn-out. As for myself, I'm getting just a little tired of writing Lynn's reports as well as my own.

I prefer to think of my feelings about the current situation as a variation on a theme of role conflict rather than a feminist litmus test. That's why I refuse to feel guilty, any more than I will allow myself to bury the issue. But it is something to be grappled with, and resolution seems to elude me. Like Hester Prynne, I believe I should go about my business, but with a mark of moral sin visible to the world for having had feelings which belie my value system. Perhaps my breastplate should read, like the lapel button of a few years ago, "My Karma Ran Over My Dogma."

I know there has to be an answer to this dilemma, and no doubt a sound feminist analysis of the problem will put me right.

But in the meantime, can anybody out there tell me how to get my work done?

Mentoring

S he sits before me in her well-tailored suit and white blouse, perfectly poised and full of hope. Her neatly styled hair and subdued makeup enhance a pretty face that not very many years ago would have been called adorable in a school photo. She is full of energy, confidence, and curiosity, and chomping at the bit to get on with it.

I look at her typeset resume and smile at its inflations. There's only so much you can have achieved at the ripe old age of 22. Still, it speaks to me of intellect, resourcefulness, and commitment. As I probe, I hear the voice of an emerging woman, who, like a novitiate, is driven by deep-seated beliefs and firm resolve.

She has come, she explains, because a friend of a friend told her I was someone she could talk to, and I "knew a lot." Good. The networks are working, and women are beginning to help each other.

I remember in my own experience, not all that many years ago, how women spoke of mentoring, networking. Their rhetoric was rich with promise and much embraced by those of us who'd gotten a late start in the world of work and personhood. All too often, though, the language of sisterhood led us to closed doors and cold shoulders, because the women who had "made it" were busy keeping it. Sociologically it isn't difficult to understand why. Carving out a piece of turf wasn't easy for women in the 1960's and 1970's, and holding on to it usually meant adapting to the cruel realities of competition and corporate life (which, some would charge, is a kind way of saying that women learned pretty quickly how to behave like men). But to be jobless and on the receiving end of behavior which belies women's promise to each other was a painful experience, and one which I determined never to repeat.

I have never been sorry for that resolution. I have met, befriended, and helped (I hope), some of the most splendid young women one could know. Sometimes we never meet again, but I know from their warm and honest thank you letters that I have touched them in some way, usually more because of a sympathetic ear than a job lead. Others, I remain in contact with, and so I watch with almost maternal pride as they grow and flourish. Vainly, I like to think that I may have had something to do with their success, or—more importantly—their personal growth. I am flattered when they send their friends to me, and with each new encounter, I am enriched immeasurably by the honesty and freshness and high ideals these women bring to me. Mentoring is to me a great honor and one of the privileges of being middle-aged. I consider it one of the finer rewards for "making it."

So I say to the woman before me, as I always do, "What are you really interested in?"

Like each one before her, she responds, "I want to work with people!"

Soon we move beyond that, and as she relaxes and begins to talk about who she is and what she really wants out of life, I see again a young woman full of promise, someone who gives me hope for the future, and makes me believe once more in my own ideals.

After half an hour or so, she apologizes for taking so much of my time. "I really enjoyed talking to you," she says earnestly. "Thank you!"

"The pleasure was mine," I say, wondering if she'll ever know how much I meant it.

WOMAN, THY NAME
IS STRENGTH

NEEDY WOMEN

I need to write.

Not "I like to write" or "I want to write." I need to write. This absolute need is something a lot of people still don't understand. (Freud never did. He might just as well have asked "What do women NEED?" as "What do women WANT?") My husband, for example, knows that I like to write, and that I want to write, and he is wonderfully supportive. He derives enormous pleasure when my work is published, and whenever he reads something I might have written, he says, "You could have done a better job than that!" However, he still doesn't quite understand my need to write. To him, it remains in the domain of recreation; something else that I do. Because it is not (yet) equated with very much money, he thinks of it as a hobby, an interest. He understands that I am somewhat driven ("Are you in front of that bloody computer AGAIN?"), but he would not understand (yet) if I told him that somewhere inside of me is a piece of Virginia Woolf, or Dorothy Parker, or Alice Walker. (He would probably concede Erma Bombeck.)

I know when I especially need to write, like now, because I become irritable, surly—the World's Greatest Grouch. My back aches and I'm chronically exhausted. Sometimes I even break out in a rash. My whole system goes 'tilt.' It happens to me with predictable regularity, even when I plan to 'take time off.'

Not that I don't have enough to do. When I am not writing, or thinking about writing, I am wifing, mothering, daughtering, working at my "real job," volunteering, and all the rest. But that's not the same.

For other women, it might be painting or playing music. It could be designing a dress or concocting a quiche. Perhaps it's figuring out new strategies for coping with hyperactive children or hypoactive colleagues.

The common denominator, the thing that our children and lovers and husbands and friends just can't get sometimes is this: We need to create—not just to be busy—but to be creative. The difference is rather like believing that pausing is relaxing. The former is a break, a teaser of a reward, a distraction. True relaxation is something we do to restore balance, to find our centeredness, to integrate our being into one body-soul. That—and more—is what women seek in creating. In applying our natural energy and intellect, we fight that most hideous of women's diseases—boredom—which, once internalized as "our" problem, nullifies our very spirit and makes of us non-beings—no matter how well we appear to function.

Ask any woman who has known the joy of working in a natural state of flow—that delicate balance between anxiety and boredom when all our faculties are stretched and applied to a task with such verve that time stands still and creation is power!

This act of creating is inner-directed, and we must honor it, for we have no choice. Its liberating inevitability knows no bounds, not even time.

Take this essay, for example. Somehow I found the two hours it took to write it because I simply had to. Writing it, like the proverbial slap across the face to stop mounting hysteria, has set me free to move on. It's amazing, but it works every time.

Thanks—I needed that.

COMING OUT

My friend Ellen, the Ph.D., is a 57-year-old cherub. It's not only that she's sweet and wonderful; she looks like a cherub. Her gentle, round face hides behind a fringe of bangs in a blonde dutch-boy cut which she has probably worn since she was a little girl. Ellen is also a survivor. She has lived through a husband's desertion, a son's death, an interrupted career, a jilting lover. Professor, women's leader, innovator, her next goal is to develop a curriculum which helps black and white women heal their wounds. Still, she hides behind her bangs.

Melanie is another one of my wonderful, bright, resourceful friends. Like Ellen, she is attractive and enormously appealing, even if she is slightly overweight. She had the courage, after 28 years, to leave a destructive marriage and begin a career. The first thing she did, based on a vision of women's independence, was to found a conference center for women. Now a fund raiser and community development expert, her current projects include a South African interracial arts program and the planning of a feminist conference on women's mental health. One of the interesting things about Melanie is that every time she adds a project, she adds a pound. One woman's haircut is another woman's hips.

My own guise is less visible. Despite an eclectic set of successes, I hide beneath an overriding cynicism which occasionally emerges as sardonic wit. But girth or mirth, the play is the same, clearly a symptom of the Hidden Woman Syndrome.

I had a sudden attack of HWS just the other day (which is why I am writing this essay). Meeting with a group of women for what might have been seen as a Power Lunch if it were not for our genuine talents and gentle natures, I was suddenly seized by the gnawing feeling that I wasn't REALLY one of them. I mean, here was a set of women whose collective credentials and experience would knock the socks off any headhunter. Their humor, energy, and intellect were a joy. They seemed to get a kick out of me too. Despite their compliments about my own achievements as we explored how we might work together, the old if-only-they-knew-what-a-charlatan-I-really-am feeling crept up my neck and stuck in my throat. Afterwards, by way of complimenting her, I confessed to one of them. "You too?" she exclaimed. "My God, I was feeling exactly the same way about you!"

I shared the experience with Ellen and Melanie, and it was then that each of us had the "aha!" experience: For Ellen, it means cutting her bangs, coming out of hiding to show her face and strut her stuff. Melanie will ultimately shed the pounds because what's behind them is worthy and wonderful and ought to be seen. And I will think about allowing skill and sharing to replace banal banter because what I have to contribute is real and perhaps even unique.

The pervasiveness of women's hiding from others, and each other, is only now becoming clear to me. So I would like to propose an antidote. As women in ancient cultures celebrated their aging through croning ceremonies, I propose that we modern women, as rich in talent and creativity as our older sisters were in wisdom and foresight, throw ourselves one helluva "Coming Out" party. At this party, we will make our own music and dance to our own rhythms. We won't have dance cards. There will be no shrinking violets, no "wallflowers." Instead we will sing and stomp and sway and not be afraid that "we" are not "they." We will shed our shawls of facade and know that we are, each of us, as sound in our footing and our flair as the next. We will take pride together in our achievements and find courage from each other in our endeavors. Most important, we will see that the time has definitely come to change partners and dance.

COMPANY WOMEN

M y friend is the perfect wife. She irons her husband's shirts and packs them for him when he goes on a business trip. She dutifully serves him nutritious meals on the nights that he is home, and never expects that he will take a turn at cleaning up. When he needs to work late at night, she ensures that he is not disturbed. Her schedule as an artist is always made to accommodate his. So I was surprised one day when she blurted out, "If only I could believe in God and the corporation, everything would be all right!"

This outburst had been prompted, as it turned out, by a Christmas toast to the wives of the executives with whom her husband works. The number one corporate jock had publicly thanked the wives "who play their part in the company's success" by always being on call to pack their husband's bags and drive them to the airport. None of the wives revealed their outrage at the ludicrous suggestion that they were willfully in collusion with corporate practices that were nearly destroying them and their families. Only later in the women's room did one of them confess that she had nearly left the room during the toast. All of them acknowledged privately, and bitterly, that while company stocks were going up, spousal psyches were heading for a colossal crash.

The phenomenon is not unique to the corporate world. In a similar scenario, another friend, married to an international public sector type for almost 20 years, confided that when she finally decided to pursue separation, it was as much her husband's employer as her husband that she wanted to divorce. Her explanation was forceful. The genius of the organization, she said, was in the benefits package. "It really is the gilded cage," she explained. "They co-opt you with all kinds of material benefits until your personal life becomes a micro-

cosm of the institution. After a while, you forget who you are
and why you first wanted to be there. You withdraw from any
organic involvement."

This was particularly critical to her since her husband's work,
and their mutual interest as young adults, had been community development. Over the years, she had seen the gradual
relinquishing of the value system which had first drawn her to
the man she married. Like his coworkers, he began to abandon
the qualitative aspects of his work when he intuited that it
would be organizationally unpopular. His early motivation
had become diverted to the improvement of his own quality of
life, fully if not overtly endorsed by the institution for which
he worked. "An incredible pattern of consumption began to
be obvious," my friend recalls. "All of these guys turned 50,
ran out and bought IBM's, VCR's, and BMW's. Life became
defined by three-letter status symbols!" Others carried it even
further. While publicly lavishing their wives with furs, first-
class travel, and the latest in gadgetry, many were subcon-
sciously projecting their own sense of failure and disappointment onto them, so that these women—who couldn't quite
articulate the problem—knew incontrovertibly that they were
responsible for it.

Listening to these two women made me remember what
suddenly seemed like a sea of others. Whether they had
remained married or not, those who were talking were basi-
cally saying the same thing. Some were more articulate than
others; some more in tune with their own feelings. But all of
them felt trapped by appearances and agendas which they had
not set. Somehow they had been co-opted into a "culture" in
which they felt like strangers trying to adapt. As in any culture,
reward came with learning the language, refining the art of
accepted courtesies, and studiously avoiding the committing
of offenses. The twist in this particular culture, however, was
that the reward constituted the punishment. Realizing this had
sent some of these company women in search of an "exit visa."
For the others, the only respite resided in the company of
women.

WATCHING OUR GARDENS GROW

In Alice Walker's fine collection of essays, *In Search of Our Mother's Gardens*, she tells us, in the piece from which the title is taken, of the importance of a little garden in her mother's life. Amidst the poverty and barrenness of daily existence, that small patch of colorful flowers—so carefully and lovingly laid out and tended to—was her mother's way of bringing order and beauty to life.

We need to tend another kind of garden now, for there is an urgent planting and sowing that must take place amidst a moral poverty and barrenness that threatens our own daily landscape. That emptiness may not even be visible, until we begin to fill it with a new social order and a new sense of what is beautiful. Like Alice Walker's mother, we may have to dedicate space in our lives, and give to that space time, affection, and action. But unlike her, we don't need a green thumb. Our tools will not be rakes and hoes. We will be able to build our gardens year-round, night or day, wherever we are. We will be members of a special breed of gardener, farming the land in a new way to bring from it all that is best in its roots. And when our garden blooms, no one will know who we were; but it won't matter.

One of these special gardeners, a sort of Earth Mother, is my friend Clara Schiffer. Clara is retired from the government now, and she should be taking a long-earned rest. But instead she is "gardening" like mad, planting seeds here, there, and everywhere—just as she has always done. When she learned that pregnant women in the jails of Washington, DC, were being forced to labor and to deliver their babies handcuffed, Clara acted to put an end to that incredible inhumanity. When she realized that children were being dangerously exploited in the workplaces of this country (including the fast food chains),

she planted a seed in the ear of just the right person on Capitol
Hill; soon after, congressional hearings were held.   Clara is
even responsible for a bench being placed at the bus stop at the
National Institutes of Health.   "A lot of old people wait there,"
she once explained to me.   "It's outrageous that there was no
place for them to sit!"   Clara always knows just where to dig,
how far to drop the seed, and how often it needs watering.

   I thought about Clara recently at a dinner party, when I
decided to "take a risk," as one of my favorite "gardeners"
likes to say. The group was comprised largely of my husband's
business colleagues and their spouses, and the reason the
things I said were risky is that one of the conventions of the
conservative organization represented is that "wives don't
make waves." This conflicts with one of my own conventions:
gardeners must garden. Inevitably, the conversation got around
to something in which the role of women was considered a
lively conversation piece. (This bait is frequently tossed at me
since I am known to be, God help us, a feminist—which I
suspect is thought of as once-removed from an agitator.) This
time, when I settled into the trenches to take up my position,
the "enemy" was my husband's colleague, a genteel and
highly likeable sort of man who always makes a most articulate
case for continued patriarchy. That is why he is so troublesome
(if not dangerous), and that is why we gardeners must be ever
vigilant for fertile soil, and always poised for planting. The
dialogue that ensued isn't worth recounting; it is simply variation on a theme. What is important is that when it was over,
and I had crawled out of my lonely trench as disheveled and
exhausted emotionally as if I'd just plowed an enormous corn
field, I knew without a doubt that I had indeed planted a seed.
It was in the stunned expressions of the men (who thought the
conversation "very stimulating"), and it was in the spirit of the
gardener-wives, one of whom said to me, "keep up the fight!"

   It is a fight that won't be fought with boxing but with gardening gloves. And whether the seeds are for labor reform, or
women's rights, or environmental integrity, or humane health
care, or any other social justice issue, we must be there.

It is the least we can do for Alice Walker's mother, and for Clara Schiffer, and for all the gardeners before us whose labors have given to each of us beauty and safety and that to which we are entitled. It is surely the very best way to watch our gardens grow, and to give to the world the sweetest of bouquets.

GET THE MESSAGE?

The marketing moguls of Madison Avenue who write copy for clients in the health sector must be working overtime lately. Perhaps I'm just taking notice more acutely since so many ads appear to be aimed at aging women. But as one perched exactly on the midpoint of the forties decade, they make my graying hair curl!

The first ad that comes to mind appeared a while back in a medical magazine of the sort that doctors leave in their waiting rooms. Opposite a full-page photograph of an unusually attractive mid-life woman whose face was contorted by depression and despair, the copy—aimed at physicians—read "When she can't take control, you can." The ad promoted an estrogen replacement therapy (ERT) for menopausal women. Then, not long ago, I spotted an ad for calcium supplements used to help prevent osteoporosis, this time directed at women consumers. The print copy wasn't bad, but as usual, a picture is worth a thousand words. In a continuous frame of sequences showing a women progressing from approximately 35 to 70 years of age, only the first frame portrayed a healthy, happy, normal female. The rest presented a perverse distortion of the aging process, depicting a stooped, sullen, unkempt, and unattractive woman.

Not all offensive and erroneous advertising is geared to the over-forty set. Recently I happened to see an ad for a "post-menstrual disposable douche." It touted a "natural cleansing ingredient for more effective cleansing and deodorizing . . . so you can start your month feeling fresher." This ad was particularly insidious and enraging. Any woman who has ever read anything about the female reproductive cycle knows that her body is undergoing a natural cleansing through the process of menstruation, so that she will, without the pharmaceutical intervention, start the month "fresher." The suggestion that she needs to be deodorized and cleansed dates back to the ancient myth that women are polluted and therefore untouchable during their menses. Surely this is not a message we want to resurrect for our daughters.

All of this reminds me of the battles fought by those of us who were active in the women's health movement during the 1970's. We made some fine progress in those days, blowing the whistle on unnecessary hysterectomies and C-sections, paving the way for options in the treatment of breast cancer, challenging researchers on the safety and efficacy of drugs and diagnostics, and changing the image of women in the media. We lost a few causes, to be sure. But must we dig the trenches all over again to do battle with those who would so perversely co-opt and manipulate our issues and image?

The concern does not stop with messages aimed at selling to women, nor does the concern end with our country or our profit culture. Media messages are being developed all over the world as part of health education and communication efforts aimed at a variety of health-related behaviors. Many of these messages concentrate on fertility reduction. Some of them are deeply disturbing. One filmed message in an African country depicts a woman being beaten by her husband for being pregnant again. Another Asian print message admonishes women that if they are continually pregnant, they will be fat and unattractive, forcing their husbands to stray.

All of these examples point to one message: Women are victims—victims of the aging process, victims of their own reproductive capacity, indeed, victims of gender. If they are clever, they will learn to be smart victims: to consume, cleanse, contracept, concede—but never to control.

Perhaps if the market researchers of Madison Avenue and elsewhere adhered to the principle of consumer preference and perception, they would soon realize that women want to be told the truth in an adult manner, and that they perceive the perpetrators of archaic myths about women as insulting profiteers at best and obsessed with their own machismo at worst. Maybe the Madison Avenue boys and their ilk need to take a good look at their own image, if they can cope with the consequences. Get the message?

THE LOCKER ROOM LAW BOYS

They come replete with top of the line polyester plaid suits and pinky rings in assorted sizes and shapes. Their offices are tastefully overdecorated and their secretaries always sound like they come from somewhere south of Chapel Hill. They are the jocks of real estate law, and a recent encounter in the buying and selling of our house was a revelation.

I entered the transaction feeling like the proverbial Cheshire Cat, having gone to the mat with the mortgage company and won on the issue of lending rates. But I was quickly put in place by our buyer's lawyer. "The only reason you got that extension was because you were a bitch," he said cheerfully. The styrofoam cup in my hand shook. "That's why we like to send women in to deal with contractors and banks. They're so bitchy, it works every time!" he grinned.

"I prefer to think of myself as an effective consumer," I said with a plastic smile.

"Oh, no, it's being a bitch that works," he assured me.

"Well, perhaps we should get on with it," said my husband nervously.

Just as things were progressing smoothly, our buyer's lawyer piped up again. "I think we need a penalty clause for failure to vacate—say $175 a day?"

"But we're going to vacate," my husband and I assured him, "There's absolutely no reason for us not to vacate."

There ensued after this the most prolonged debate on a moot point that I have ever had to endure. Their lawyer fought it out with our lawyer, both of whom seemed to have forgotten that buyer and seller were still present. It was a classic sparring match, clearly sport for the participants if not the spectators. In the most erudite and articulate fashion, the two fenced around the non-issue with eloquent hostility. Finally, we ruled it a draw by agreeing to the potential penalty. Both lawyers seemed disappointed that the game had come to an end—but not without one further mindboggling ritual.

After the papers had all been signed in an atmosphere of subdued rage and mild confusion, the most amazing thing of all happened. Our lawyer, having just moments ago hurled a vitriolic attack at their lawyer, suddenly jumped up and gave him a huge and spontaneous bear hug. "You shoulda held us up for $250 a day!" he screeched. "Great job! I love ya!" Their lawyer responded with a resounding pat on our lawyer's behind.

Suddenly it all made sense: the teakwood table is the weekday playing field. Whether it's racquetball or real estate, the game's the same, and it's the playing that counts. Boys will be boys, and all that. But then, what do I know? I'm just a silly bitch.

GIVING UP THE RAG

W hen I was nine years old, my mother, a victim of the "We'll just take out the carriage and leave the play-pen" fraternity, had a hysterectomy. Conventional wisdom in those days dictated that at the first premenopausal irregularity the female reproductive organs were dispensed with. I distinctly remember sitting on the stairs, my head in my hands, regretting bitterly that I had been born a girl, and terrified by what inevitably lay ahead. As I approached my own entry into womanhood, a stream of other terrors made their way into my subconscious, fueled by the whispered sharing of older girls and a variety of ominous magazine articles—usually conspicuously available in the doctor's waiting room.

Fortunately for women of my generation, and thanks largely to the women's health movement of the 1970's, most of the mythology-driven attitudes and practices aimed at "normalizing" the reproductive cycle have been put to rest. But a few hard core neanderthals persist and need to be reminded that, unlike our mothers, we are not, literally or figuratively, going to take it lying down.

We've gotten too smart. We know now, through the sharing of our own reality, that middle age and older can be a time of invigorating energy and freedom as we have never known it. Many of us, to the chagrin of our fading male counterparts, take up artistic, business, or service endeavors with talented fervor. Contrary to the beliefs of those who cling to Victorian notions of femininity, we do not fall into a fretful malaise at the end of our "biological significance" (as my daughter's high school biology teacher puts it). Some of us celebrate it.

I, for one, not having had to face the very real issue of the biological clock, welcome the normal end of a very annoying monthly event. I mean, let's face it. It's been a nuisance

crawling onto our "Mickey Mouse mattresses" every 28 days
or so, ever watchful for that awkward accident at exactly the
wrong time. Our husbands and lovers tire of competing with
a tampon, and it's no fun for us to keep apologizing for being
premenstrual, menstrual, or perimenstrual. It will be wonderful to pack a suitcase without consulting the calendar and to
give up the midnight search for an all-night pharmacy. And
I plan to work out exactly what I've invested in "feminine
hygiene products" over the course of some 40 years, and to
make an equal and immediate contribution toward pampering
myself.

Anyone who thinks this is an odd form of "involutional
melancholia," as our menopausal years used to be labeled,
needs to be reminded that times have changed. Young girls no
longer fear their womanhood: they welcome it. Like their
mothers, they now embrace maturity with all its gifts. After
all, it's simply part of the life cycle.

On Reaching Middle Age

Today I turned 45. In the vernacular of my daughter, it's an awesome event. I mean, you can hardly get more middle-aged than that. In fact, unless the gods are very good to me, I may have passed my own midpoint some time ago without even stopping to think about it. Having realized this milestone of "middlescence," I'm thinking about it now. I find it a kind of "on the one hand, on the other hand" appraisal.

For example, I appreciate the wisdom of the sardonic sage who said, "I hate the thought of growing old, until I consider the alternative." I recognize a certain maturity and intelligence for which I feel proud now and again. I do not, however, appreciate that my intellectual growth spurts occur in inverse correlation to a spreading girth and a thinning head of hair.

I've also noticed with some chagrin that men and women age differently. It's not just the notion that men with graying temples are wise and sexy while women are simply past their prime—my days in the women's movement got me past that—but that men reward what women re-examine. My husband lavished himself with a BMW and a betamax when he turned 50. "I deserve it!" he crowed like a proud peacock. With five years yet to go, I've already begun to question our lifestyle, even though I know "we've worked hard," and "no one ever gave us anything." I've also begun to think about such things as wills and who should take care of what. Every time I ask my husband where he would like his final resting place to be, he laughs nervously and talks about getting a compact disk player.

But I find midlife reflections comforting. They bring me back to important reference points in life. I remember, for instance, the first guiding principle I chose to adopt in adolescence: to thine own self be true. Shortly afterwards, I discovered that "change is the only reality." These two philosophies, so elegantly simple, have remained for me the essential knowledge.

In fact, with every passing year, simplicity seems to be the key. In a way, it's what my acupuncturist friend calls "letting go"—the mellowing out of middle age. I think of it now in this way: if in the cosmic view of things it doesn't matter, screw it. Know what's important. Be honest. And no matter how bad it gets, it can't stay that way.

Maybe it's understanding that I know this that made my daughter say this morning, "You shouldn't be upset because you're 45. That just means you're wiser. You should be happy!"

She's right, my smart, savvy teenager with the strange vocabulary.

But, on the other hand . . . I wouldn't mind learning a few things all over again. After all, I deserve it.

MARCHING TO THE MIDLIFE DRUMMER

When I was a girl, a lot of things my popular and witty teenage sister said just didn't seem to make sense. "You've gotta learn to play the game," she counseled as I reached the age of bras, braces, and boys. "Don't be so honest! You don't have to let them know how smart you are!" I couldn't put my finger on it at the time, but the notion that one had to be less to be more was decidedly confusing to me.

Adults had another theme which was equally troubling. "Don't set your sights so high. You'll only be disappointed," said my immigrant parents, as general commentary. More specifically, they concerned themselves with security. "She has such high standards," they worried as I entered my college years. "What she needs is a job she can fall back on." It didn't seem to matter what that was, as long as it happened in an environment of eligible bachelors and regular paychecks.

Dishonesty and diminished hopes didn't seem the route to a fulfilled future, but in the fifties, no feminist analysis existed to explain why I felt the psychological equivalent of sick to my stomach a good part of the time. But, being the good girl that I was, I tried desperately to "win." (After all, my "successful" sister was married to an engineer by the age of 21, and surely my parents knew best; they had survived the depression.) Off I went to college to become a teacher (the standard fallback position for good Jewish girls), intending at the same time to master the art of being coy.

Somehow, I just couldn't make it work. Like a dreamwalker, I was leading someone else's life. I didn't want to be a teacher, and I didn't want to marry any old doctor, lawyer, or Indian chief—at least not yet. There was too much world out there—too much to see, to do, to be. So I committed the ultimate heresy: I dropped out of school before getting either a B.S., or—more importantly—the coveted MRS., and went to New York to explore life's options.

Life in Manhattan in the early 1960's was still vibrant and viable for a young woman. I had a good administrative job, fine friends, and a strong sense of adventure. While my contemporaries married, had babies, and settled down in the suburbs, I enjoyed travel, romance, and employment in Europe—always with the nagging feeling that I was doing something wrong and they were terribly right. Ultimately, I completed my education, married a sweet man, and had two lovely children, all of which has added to my continually expanding persona. But it was a long time before I could trust my own reality.

The point of this exposition is not biography. It is transition. Connection. Security in self. I recall my youthful experience and perceptions because they are part of me now, as I look complacency straight in the eye once more, reflecting again on "middlescence." (How foolish of me to think that "midlife crisis" is a one-time event.)

I review my status. Impressive job, good income. "Don't rock the boat!" I hear my father say. But I feel the vines of boredom wrapping around my heart. And I know that if I don't cut free of them, they will choke the life out of me, even though I will continue to breathe dully in and out. Not for me still, security, playing the game. No, no! I have "miles to go before I sleep," as the good poet Robert Frost put it.

I know that sooner or later, I will create another me. I will seek a challenge, fueled by aspiration, while others cry "Enough already!" I dream of how to invent my next iteration in which I want to be Jane Austen-Beryl Markham-Margaret Bourke-White, recording my era while living the good life in a splendid place. Maybe I will board a tramp steamer in my blue jeans with only a suitcase and my computer. Life is rich with material. Such fantasies are a good thing. They keep us alive, in touch with our potential. We should never apologize for them, or bury them, no matter how numbing the norms.

Growth must no longer be a lonely experience, something

to be secreted or abandoned because others may find our truths strange. As we grapple with discovery and enrichment, self and personhood, our own reality stands as Exhibit A. We are that we are. It is one of the gifts of maturity.

Women celebrated this gift in ancient times with croning rituals honoring older women for their wisdom and spiritual power. Great writers and artists have encouraged the quest. Goethe wrote ''Now let me dare to open wide the gate, Past which (wo)men's steps have ever flinching trod.''

It is within each of us to make that journey. Unlike the days of our growing up, we needn't worry about the rules of the game. After all, we've got the chips, and the next move is really ours.

WORRYING LESS AND ENJOYING IT MORE

I've been worrying a lot lately, and while it might sound per-
verted, I'm thoroughly enjoying it. That's because it's trivia
I'm worrying about. For the first time in my life, I am learning
to allow myself the luxury of obsessing over matters which in
the cosmic view of things don't matter a jot. For example,
when we moved recently I spent days devoted to choosing
wallpaper and fabric and wondering if they would match. I
hardly gave a second thought to whether we could actually
afford the extravagance. This was an entirely new experience
for me. Formerly, I only permitted myself to focus on matters
of life and death. God knows, there are enough concerns in
this category to fill a lifetime. But somehow, with the mellowing out of middle age, comes the sense that we women have
earned the right to let go of disaster as the only realm in which
we may rightfully anguish. Where is it written, after all, that
we must suffer to live?

This great insight has led me to another: Women suffer
depression for the same reason they are subject to prolapsed
bladders. We are always going to do (or take on) "just one
more thing."

Well, I for one have decided actively and consciously to reject
that female moral imperative. I vow from this day forward to
worry about anything that strikes my fancy, or (ah, revolution)
not to worry at all. No longer am I willing to let others two-
thirds my age with one-tenth the experience—like bosses and
physicians—suggest what might be worthy of my worry time.
From now on I will decide if, and when, to ponder and pace.
No frown shall furrow my brow without my full consent.

This promise has led to some great moments. A friend and
soul-sister with whom I shared my new resolve lit up with
understanding when I told her that I was dedicating myself to

this new philosophy. She had recently come to the same insight.

"The time we waste," she laughed, "worrying about all the wrong things!"

Amen.

CHANGE

M arx may have been right about some people when he de-clared religion the opiate of the masses. Speaking strictly as an individual, though, my addiction is to something quite different. I get high on change. My credo is more along the lines of "variety is the spice of life." I don't mean this in any hedonistic sense. It's not only that I like change—I positively need it to survive. That's why I have felt such an affinity with that wise old Greek Heraclitus ever since I was fourteen. It was then that I discovered his simple but sage proclamation: "Change is the only reality." Soon after that, Shakespeare's pearl—"To thine own self be true"—came to my attention. The two wisdoms seemed irrevocably linked in my case.

Being honest about who I was meant accepting the inevita-bility of change in my life. That insight went a long way in getting me over the guilt I sometimes felt about "needing a fix." It explained a lot about the things I did, or didn't do, when measured against other people's norms. For example, it helped me explain to my father, among others, why I was exploring Europe while other young women my age were meticulously matriculating. (It also worked in the inverse when I completed my formal education long after everyone else had mastered their masters.) Honoring change meant that, despite growing up in a depression mentality household, I could give away an article of clothing just because I was tired of it. Eventually I even worked up to buying myself a piece of costume jewelry now and then just for the hell of it—although that took a lot of guts. I would even venture to say that my compulsion for neatness and order stems from my need for change, for if things are in chaos, how does one ever know if they've changed?

Still, it's not easy. After all, we live in a highly regularized world. We are encouraged at some level—subliminal though it may be—to feel devoted to our home town, attracted to only one mate, loyal in the long term to our employer. I consider my home town a nice place, and while I've been married (and faithful) to one lovely man for 18 years, I can't say that I'm any more virtuous than Jimmy Carter—who, you will recall, publicly admitted that he lusted after women other than his wife occasionally. As for employers, I have spent five years at the same institution, and for me, that is utter longevity. Quite soon, I am sure, I will need a new and formidable challenge. Otherwise, I will once again be squaring off with boredom, which I firmly believe is a woman's disease, just as potent, uncomfortable, and threatening as such nemeses as osteoporosis and endometriosis.

Gender is an issue in all of this. That became clear to me some time ago when my husband had nearly reached the breaking point because of job stress. In the middle of the night, having been awakened by his moaning and lamentations, I counseled him to consider making a change. He looked at me blankly. "What else could I do?" he asked, childlike. The next day when I thought more about it, I came up with what I considered to be some pretty good ideas. He resisted. Suddenly I realized that there is a fundamental difference between men and women. It isn't just that men are conditioned from the start to revere institutions—among which they consider their own sacrosanct—but that they do not know how to handle change, nor do they seek it: quite to the contrary, they avoid it like the plague. The safety of routine is a comfort to them. They consider boredom an acceptable consequence of adulthood. For women, on the other hand, half the thrill of being where you are is getting there; the other half is figuring out where you go from here. The thrill of a good challenge is what motivates our inherent creative spirit, and revs up our resourcefulness. Our energy is renewed by change. We are always becoming. We make our lives happen.

I didn't understand this when I was younger. Consequently I often felt aberrant, in spite of Heraclitus. With age and maturity, however, I can admit now that I like being addicted to change. It is a natural state of affairs, the art of being, or perhaps the art of being female. I approach change with a kind of religious fervor, so maybe Marx was right after all. It's just that each of us has our own icon. And on mine, the image is ever subject to change.

REFLECTIONS

On The Art Of Letters

I begin my daily vigil at 10:58 a.m. At 11:03 I rise to pace at the window. Finally, up the road the slow rumble of the little white truck signals his imminent arrival: The Mailman Cometh!

Mail has always been a high point of my day, even before I was a writer, and my perceived value to the world arrived daily in "SASEs" and assorted legal-sized envelopes. I have often marveled at those people who can cavalierly toss the postman's offerings on their desk or into a drawer unopened, perhaps for days at a time. Don't they wonder what they are missing, tucked in between those frivolous bits of junk mail? Don't they think that someone might have sent a kind word, perhaps an invitation, a photo, a postcard from some exotic and worldly place?

Over the years, I have been courted and consoled by mail. I have been co-opted on occasion—and even condemned—but most of all I have been cared about enough that someone has taken the time to put pen to paper, to think about what to say, and usually, how to say it. How easily, in our byte-sized lives, we have been willing to give that up!

Sometimes I think about what it must have been like to live in the days when the post was a lifeline, one's primary contact with the outside world; a time when people wrote to each other with elegance and precision and subtlety; a time when social convention precluded other forms of communion. I can imagine, for example, Charlotte Brontë, in her remote and chilling Haworth Village, waiting, waiting, for word from London about her manuscript. And then at last! It comes! Perhaps the news is not good, but the correspondence from her editor, erudite and committed, is a gift that day—one that will give sustenance to her and her sisters as they sit in the lonely Parsonage, writing

for themselves, and for the world long afterwards. What was
it like, in the days of "Cyrano de Bergerac," to receive, hand-
delivered, epistolary evocations of unrequited love? How
wonderful it must have been for the aspiring writer Franz
Kappus to receive in 1903 from the unmet poet Rainer Rilke a
letter full of encouragement signed "Yours faithfully and with
all sympathy."

The beauty and value of letters are not solely the domain of
public and well-known figures, although they are a joy to read
and give meaning to the lives and work of the authors and their
recipients. Letters are also for ordinary mortals. They give us
hope and courage. They connect us to our world and help us
to understand it. They provide a way to process our lives, not
in isolation as a diary or journal might, but in camaraderie and
with compassion. Patty Lamb and Joyce Hohlwein knew this
when they corresponded from their college years through
midlife—a communication captured in the collection called *Touch-
stones*. Not that the correspondence was brilliant, or that the
two women were even totally likeable, but oh, the strength and
friendship in that sharing!

This sharing is a phenomenon that I know and cherish, and
on this day I am not disappointed by the treasures in my
mailbox. There is a letter from my unseen friend Catherine in
Wyoming, whom I "met" through one of my women writers'
newsletters. I feel on the strength of only a few letters between
us that Catherine is a deep and good friend, a thinking, feeling,
honest human being—a wise old soul who gives me the gift of
contemplation. There is a note from my soulmate, Sue, in
Chicago. Ever too busy to write much, there is nonetheless
such an essence in the few words shared that we are connected
at once in a way that both of us will laugh about later. And
there, with its colorful foreign stamp peeping out at me like a
crown jewel, is a letter from my African friend whom I had the
good fortune to meet one day in Malawi. He—and his beautifully crafted letters—never cease to amaze me and bring me
great joy. I am humbled by his intellect; awed by his knowledge of the world; and immeasurably enriched by his reflec-

tions. On this day, he writes of literature and music, and of our correspondence: "It is more steady than some of my close friends here at home, and I cherish it. Is it not a shame for people to miss this fundamental aspect of life?"

It is indeed, my friend. For, as John Donne wrote in a letter of his own 400 years ago, "more than kisses, letters mingle souls; For, thus friends absent speak."

FREEDOM

It started with the television docudrama on the Berlin Wall. There were the recreated scenes of people jumping out of windows, being impaled on barbed wire, getting shot in the back with one foot over the wall. The image that lingered in my mind for days and caused me to tear up every time I thought about it was the failed attempts of the American GI to get his East Berlin girlfriend out. Surely, we thought, he gets her out: it's only a movie. But he never did, and so she became a symbol for all the others caught in that repressive regime in the space of a single sinister night not so very long ago.

Then there was the radio interview with the doctor who serves a refugee community just outside Lebanon. Trapped by his own commitment within a ghetto of despair, he labors under appalling and primitive conditions. He will not leave because the others cannot leave.

Later, a young Iranian woman came to see me in search of work. She was one of the lucky ones: at least she was out. Her friends back home—most of them teachers or nurses—were trapped in a situation not of their making and certainly not to their liking. She told me that the nurses had a better chance because they could volunteer to go to the front where they might meet a soldier to marry. That wouldn't get them out of Iran, but it would give them a modicum of security.

Shortly afterwards, I traveled to Burma on business—an act of mobility that in itself began to seem ludicrous. There I met a lovely couple who had lost everything under the government's nationalization program. They wanted to emigrate but the prospect seemed dim. Visas are not granted to husbands and wives at the same time, nor for one in the absence of the other.

On my return journey, I made a transit stop in Singapore. The only person I really talked to there was the taxi driver. His lack of freedom to leave home—even briefly—wasn't impaired by politics. It was the yoke of poverty that kept him confined to his country. Of course, relative to the others, his situation was hopeful. But in reality, it seemed unlikely that he would ever see more distant shores.

This sudden barrage of stories and scenarios put me in touch with a whole range of freedoms that we take for granted. For me, mobility and freedom of speech rank high. Physical or psychological limitations are more rapidly soul destroying to me than any of the more outrageous oppressions. But there is also freedom from illness and disease, and freedom from hunger. (Our mothers understood this when they told us to remember the starving children.) There is the freedom one feels with warmth and shelter. And certainly, there is freedom in being truly loved.

Clearly there are personal freedoms too, for which each of us is responsible. There is the cleansing freedom to be angry and the freedom to change our minds; the freedom to fail, and to try again. We are free to disagree, or to endorse. We are, each in the privacy of our selves, free to concur or to censure. We are free to love, to be creative each in our own way, to give warmth, spiritual shelter, and psychological mobility to our soul mates. It is these very freedoms that no one can take away unless we are willing to relinquish them. And it is by these freedoms—as witnessed by those whose spirits have so miraculously survived a plethora of political repressions over the ages—that we live, and that we defy that which would destroy us. For as long as we willfully and passionately cast off the mental boundaries that limit our humanity and individual being, we are free—even in the clutter and confinement of our daily lives.

The woman from East Berlin, perhaps not long after she had married the local baker and given birth to a daughter, came to understand this. The doctor in Lebanon continues to take sustenance from those he serves. The women in Iran, like the family in Burma, support each other, and find what joy they can while waiting for a future they may yet help to shape. And the taxi driver in Singapore travels the globe in his mind's eye through the pictures painted for him by his worldly passengers.

Each of them, like countless millions of others, has made a separate peace, grounded in the freedom of their own personhood. And for that, at least, one must be thankful.

THE FINE ART OF EGO BADGING

O f all the characters I remember from my days as a social worker some years ago, one whom I recall most vividly was a young man who came to the day care center where I worked. Having duly noted that all of us on staff wore name-and-title tags, and being astute enough to realize that the practice was partly aimed at demonstrating that "we" were not "they," he soon took to wearing his own tag. Under his name, he had written in bold and proud letters, "Psychiatric Patient." Now there was a guy who understood ego-stroking, impaired though his own might have been.

I thought of him again recently when I attended a national public health convention that draws about 10,000 people. Not only was this august group named and titled, but their various badges sported colored ribbons bright enough to give new meaning to the term "rainbow coalition": green for member, red for speaker, blue for exhibitor, and so on. For those lucky enough to be all of the above, a name badge worn on the lapel like the proudest of military ribbons served as nothing less than a neon sign flashing "Status!"

For some reason—which I suspect has to do with the inbred elitism of their profession—medical types are big on this sort of thing. They've institutionalized a whole set of accoutrements and behaviors designed to put you in your place, and identify theirs. Why, for example, is it necessary for "docs" to cruise the halls of hospitals with stethoscopes cavalierly flung around their necks? Do social workers, lab techs, and other assorted ancillaries really need to wear those white lab coats with their names embroidered on the pocket? It's bad enough that everyone from x-ray technicians to orderlies jump into green surgical scrubs at the drop of a hat. Notice, please, that this variation on a theme of status-dressing occurs in inverse correlation to patient-chic, which consists of hospital gowns guaranteed to neuter and nullify faster than you can say pass the thermometer.

Not that the medical profession has an exclusive on the status market. I happen to spend a lot of time in Power Town, USA (otherwise known as Washington, DC), and I can attest personally to the briefcase hierarchy. I also know of offices where the color and size of an ashtray is a dead give-away for income bracket and flow chart position. No doubt every sphere—from the entertainment industry to the evangelical movement—has its own status symbols and stroking system.

The question is: Why? Is it fundamental to human nature that we be labeled, categorized, and put in little boxes (or big ones) depending on where we fit in the scheme of things? Does it reflect the time in which we live—a time in which we are judged more by what we do than how we do it, driven by competition rather than motivation, symbolized by the equivalent of designer name tags?

I suspect the answer lies somewhere in the middle, and deep in the collective psyche. But it's intriguing to contemplate what life would be like if all of us—including the Emperor—wore no clothes. One thing is certain and comically reassuring: We'd have nowhere to pin the name tags! Ironically, and ideally, that could make ego a great equalizer.

THE CURSE OF OPTIONS

"Free will, I find, is a terrible burden," claimed a rather pathetic character in a novel I read once. The phrase struck me when I read it and stayed with me over time. Only recently I remembered it during an after school emergency call from my daughter. "What should I do?" she wailed into the phone. "I don't know whether to try out for the school play or for the volleyball team!"

The whole day had been like that. From the trivia of choosing clothes in the morning to the trauma of career decisions with potentially monumental impact in the afternoon, I felt dizzied with the challenge of choice. By the time I crawled into bed, my husband wondered if I was ill. "It's the curse," I mumbled. "I thought you had that last week," he said. "Options!" I muttered, leaving him to drift into bewildered sleep.

Not only have my daughter and I had reason to agonize recently over the realm of possibility in our respective lives, with all the attendant stressors; but it seems to me that suddenly many of my friends and colleagues are also growing increasingly twitchy over life's offerings.

Most of them, like myself, are passionately committed to change and choice. We want everything from our insurance plans to our vacation itineraries cafeteria style. None of us would relinquish our options for anything in the world, because we know all too well that choice provides richness and texture to the fabric of life. Anyone who doubts that need only stop for a moment and ponder the lives of our sisters and brothers in developing countries who labor in exhaustion and monotony day after day after day just to stay alive and feed their offspring. The tragedy of those millions of lives is enough to make us embrace anew every choice granted to middle class and mobile inhabitants of the northern hemisphere.

That gift notwithstanding, we all know there's no free lunch. In our fast-paced world of "on the one hand, on the other hand" living, we are both blessed and cursed by the options that present themselves to us by virtue of our individual life-styles and our collective sociology. Dual career families find themselves facing what psychologists refer to as "avoidance-avoidance conflict," or no-win situations in which they must choose between careers and commuter marriages. Our kids agonize over which schools to apply to, in which extracurricular activities to engage, and to which parent to be loyal. Friendships are tested in new and undreamed of ways.

Options are also great for guilt. When I once tried to explain to my husband the dilemma of sorting out various directions I could take with my work, he sulked for days. At the heart of it—I later realized—was his feeling that I had all the options, while the obligations remained with him. (What woman with a newborn baby cannot relate to that perspective?)

None of us grappling with this new challenge to our psyches would want to go back to the days of survival and subsistence, or to the time when our world view was framed by nothing more than the tiny towns and hamlets that spawned us. Of course we will rise to the occasions, opportunities, and demands of options—the psychological equivalent, perhaps, of a "new world order." And as any psychologist (or economist) can tell you, we will pay a price—personally and socially—hoping in the end that when we have done our "cost-benefit analysis," the benefit side of the ledger is the longer of the two.

Free will and choice are indeed burdens, just as the character in the book said; but they are also blessings and gifts. So we must be sure, as we ponder the ledger sheet and grapple with the pros and cons of our own making, that we are hearing not only the lessons of psychology (and economy), but of philosophers and poets as well.

After all, given the reality of our time, that's probably our only option.

WHICH WAY TO DODGE CITY?

Judging by my zip code and all the hi-tech paraphernalia surrounding me, I live just south of the Eastern Establishment and poised on the New Age. Using current events and the headlines as indicators, however, this is the Wild West, circa 1854.

Last year, the number of homicides in Washington, DC, exceeded 300. Last month, there were 13 shootings in one night. Last week, a 12-year-old boy shot his mother to death and critically wounded his father, without even so much as a domestic dispute: he just did it one night. I doubt that Dodge City could top that even in its heyday.

Guns aren't the only means of violence to invade cities and suburbs alike, nor are family and drug wars the only source of trouble. Following the rape of a nine-year-old girl in the bathroom, a school superintendent in suburban Washington ordered that all school doors must be locked, and that children must go to the lavatories in pairs. It goes on and on, day after day after day.

As a kid, watching westerns, or listening to history lessons about the grim realities of violent times, I used to wonder how people could live with that kind of thing going on around them. Now I know. They become inured, steeled against its larger meaning, rendering the macabre mundane. Saturated by media replays, movies that spend millions to make high art of murder, and headlines that no longer scream at us unless we know the victims, norms begin to change. The intolerable becomes acceptable. I actually overheard the following conversation at a supermarket deli counter.

"Say, how's Dolores and Johnny?"

"Not so good. They had a fight and she shot him. He's dead."

"Yeah? No kiddin'? Say, where'd you say we keep the bologna?"

More poignantly, when a friend told her youngster recently that a prominent member of the community had died, the four-year-old's response was, "Who shot him?"

Where does it end?

This is not a rhetorical question: it begs to be answered, and the urgency of the reply must be felt and internalized by each of us. No longer can we delude ourselves with the complacency of "it can't happen to me." We cannot remain uninvolved, for when one of us is violated, we are each humiliated and made afraid. Somehow, before it is too late for us—individually and as a society—we must get to the heart of what is eroding our humanity, and terrifying us, no matter how hard we work to deny it. Otherwise, we are doomed to an Armageddon of our own making, and in our own time.

Even the folks in Dodge City wouldn't have settled for that.

BETRAYAL

B etrayal is a lofty theme in the hands of great writers and dramatists. When Chekhov or Shakespeare bring the act of dishonoring others into focus, it is an illuminating experience for those of us who would be voyeurs into the human mind.

But in the everydayness of our lives, betrayal is not lofty and interesting. It is ugly and cold and painful. It shows us the blemished face of those we love and trust. It arises from base motives, and a selfishness that is stunning when acted out.

Betrayal is silence when there should be support. It is a friend saying I cannot help you because I may risk hurting myself. It is the Machiavellian twisting of truth for the saving of one's own desires. It screams at us "I shall have what I want!" and mocks our trust as naiveté.

The artful betrayer lays at our feet ownership for the void. Paralyzed by what has transpired, we subscribe to that insult. From emptiness we find our way back to reality, but we are never fully restored. In that experience is a gnawing pain that stays in our souls breeding distrust and contempt. Beauty and purity are damaged forever. We search for flaws, and close in around ourselves for protection. We are forever altered. And so we are denied what might have been.

Betrayal as art may illuminate and excite us; but betrayal in life is harsh and bitter loss.

JUST SAY NO

Obviously the Madison Avenue whiz kid who came up with drug education's tag line has no children; otherwise he would understand how hard it is to "just say no." I don't mean for the kids: I mean for their parents.

My cohort seems to be having a helluva time saying "no" to its offspring, and consequently, even if peer pressure were viable at this age, it isn't there to help. I'm not sure what it is, but a lot of otherwise sensible people are serving up indulgence like it's going out of style. I know one parent who serves alcohol to her son's friends when they have a party. "We all drank a little when we were in high school," she coos. Another single father gave the house key to his sixteen-year-old son when he left for several days business. "Why not have some friends over?" he asked benevolently. (He returned home to find his booze, and his porn flicks, gone forever.) A leader in the school community recently organized a panel of parents and students to discuss substance abuse in the schools, which is—according to the kids—rampant. A week later, this same community leader let her daughter attend an unchaperoned party, knowing that before the night was over, in all likelihood, several hundred kids would convene at the house before the police arrived to break it up. "It's so hard to say 'no'," she explained, "when all the other kids get to go."

It's even harder for those parents who manage to do it. I hate being known as the hard-nosed mother in the group. It's not easy steeling myself against well-rehearsed soliloquies about my rigidity and ridiculous standards. It's painful to watch my daughter miss out on parties that her friends go to because there will be booze and bouncers, but there won't be parents. But that's the rule in this house. Because when the cops get there, they won't care whether my daughter was exercising good judgment or not. More importantly, I don't want her to find out the hard way that the situation was more than she could handle.

Ironically, I do trust her judgment—a whole lot more than I do the parents who are abdicating under peer pressure once removed. We'd all have an easier job if we just set some standards in one calm, collective voice that suggested maturity rather than muddling to our children. Make no mistake: they know when we're waffling, and they don't like it. Despite the requisite resistance to rules, authority is appreciated and makes for sound parameters while crossing over the chasm from childhood. Ask any kid whose parents never say no.

Maybe what we need is better social support systems—not for our kids—for us. We need to learn how to make good decisions and how to stick by them. We need to trust that our kids will still love us when we "deprive" them, because sometimes less really is more. Most of all, we need to remember that "the other kids"—that mystical group of empowerment—are no more, or less, than our own kids, asking someone else to go first.

IMPRESSIONS AT A PROTEST

There was no sense of a crowd at first. Walking towards the mall on that quiet, crisp Sunday felt pleasant but not extraordinary. The only hint of a happening was the proliferation of vendors' trucks lining Constitution Avenue, and of course, the police, poised on their Yamahas as if waiting for a curtain call in The Keystone Kops. Here and there, women—many in white or purple—joined each other, moving rhythmically in the same direction. Banners, some still rolled, others unfurled, began to speak to the event. "Friends for Choice," "Alice Paul Chapt. NOW, Glassboro, NJ," "Women's Medical Center of Greater Washington," "Psychologists for Free Choice," read the uniform purple, white, and yellow silk messages. Colorful and creative homemade posters, many hand lettered on cardboard, joined in. "Ronald Who?" "Jane Wyman was right!" "Girls just want to have Choices!" Buttons supported banners. "Uppity Women Unite." "I'm for Choice and I Vote." "Choice."

Suddenly the individual groups begin to merge; the momentum picks up; the sum becomes greater—much greater—than its parts. The mall is alive with something real and bonding and strong. Energy ripples through the growing mass. Over the loudspeaker, organizers announce the location of groups, assigned to invisible aisles marked by placards in a bingo game. "We're 0-2!" someone shouts, and the group follows its leader to its stake-out. The crowd continues to grow. Friendly hawkers flog ribbons, buttons, T-shirts; and organizations take advantage of the opportunity to hand out literature. Political and physical diversity reveals once again our pluralism. And still the numbers grow. Groups joke, wave greetings, applaud each other's banners. Friends meet, squealing in delight to discover a long lost, but not forgotten, sister. Toddlers in tow, often atop a dad's shoulders, watch wide-eyed the organized chaos around them. And the numbers grow. We are patient and playful, and somehow, we take shape in rows of twelve behind our respective banners. A man and woman ahead of us unfold a banner and she says laughingly to her neighbor, "Can you believe it? We have six daughters, all over the world, and here we are!"

Behind us, the Gray Panthers of Montgomery County (Maryland) line up and a cheer goes up on their behalf. Gray-haired and beaming, they represent, for many of us, the symbolic silver lining behind the cloud which threatens us again. Finally, slowly, we begin to move. Songsheets are passed out and people begin to sing or chant. Then like a river, we flow down Pennsylvania Avenue, wave upon wave upon wave, cresting past the few who have come in opposition, rolling by the tourists who stop to ask what is happening, undulating purposefully towards the Capitol. There we deliver our message, and it reverberates like the echo in a giant seashell, etched out by time, abrasion, intrusion.

When it is over, we begin to break ranks, exhausted and exhilarated. Smiling to each other, we disperse. Banners are rolled, backpacks readjusted, goodbyes shared. Walking away, I think how far we have come on this day. Then I hear a little girl of about seven say to her mother, "Mom, what's a protest?" Her mother looks at me wearily, and we smile to each other; for both of us know in that moment how very much further we have yet to go.

ORPHANS IN THE PUBLIC HEALTH WARD

"It's a hard-knock life!" according to Little Orphan Annie, who sang her heart out with peculiarly jovial affect, under the circumstances, in the Broadway musical. She was right when it comes to women and public health, but unlike the fictional Annie, activists aren't frolicking. They're frustrated.

Consider the work of Texas psychiatrist Jean Hamilton, a founder of the Institute for Research on Women's Health (IRWH). Dr. Hamilton and her colleagues continue the struggle to secure funding for women's health research begun when IRWH was started in 1984. They have cause for concern. Recently, for example, a large-scale study by the National Cancer Institute (known as the "Women's Health Trial") to investigate the relationship between fat and breast cancer was cancelled when preliminary data revealed that an adequate trial would be more costly than originally expected. "IRWH scientists believe that the fate of the WHT study is symptomatic of a larger problem, the devaluation of women's health research and the bias against spending the amount of money necessary to adequately address women's health issues," says Hamilton.

Things are not better further afield, particularly when it comes to gender bias. In India, one of the more appalling examples of this phenomenon was the creation of clinics providing sex-determination techniques aimed at female feticide. According to Darryl D'Monte of International Planned Parenthood Federation of Bombay, between 1978 and 1982, an estimated 78,000 female fetuses were aborted in India following amniocentesis. The state of Maharashtra, which has just begun to regulate the use of prenatal diagnostic techniques, has met with criticism, particularly from the medical profession. Some doctors have made the case that female feticide is preferable to bride-burning and other atrocities for the curse of being a girl-child.

Amazing as this spurious argument is, it is no surprise that it comes from a medical establishment that still views women as "incubators and child caretakers." Maternal and child health initiatives continue to focus on women only with respect to their reproductive roles, and child survival and other primary health care programs continue to count on women as unpaid extensions of the health care delivery system.

This noblesse oblige-inspired approach on the part of external change agents reflects profoundly on fundamental attitudes about women which have only rhetorically been overcome. Pushed to the limit of their patience, however, many people who purport to know better reveal neanderthal beliefs and, on occasion, amazing hostility. One senior World Bank official, wedded to the classic "biology is destiny" mindset, pontificated at a recent cocktail party that bearing and raising children was all women really wanted and what they were meant to do—a position he would never have taken on the public podium. Similarly, in a private meeting with women scientists, a senior foundation official vented his feelings, blurting out, "The trouble with all you women is that you get so emotional over your issues!"

This subliminal truth-telling is one reason that one prominent public interest fund raising professional refuses to write grants for her clients. She believes that foundation grant making is a model that replicates female dependency, paternalism, and exploitation—an important perspective to keep in mind, whether the issue is research priorities, fund raising, service delivery, or policy making. In developing new ways to meet the women's health agenda, it will be critical that we work against attitudes and practices rooted in the devaluation of women.

The time has come to put our money where our mouths are and to mouth only what is accurate and appropriate based on women's realities as they relate to public health. Maybe then, as Annie said, "the sun will come out tomorrow."

"Just Let Me Rock Her In My Arms Until She Dies"

Such was the heartbreaking plea of a young welfare mother in New York as her baby lay dying of AIDS. Her lament fell on ears deafened by a bureaucracy that ruled that she would be ineligible for benefits if she stayed with her institutionalized child. In that one swift and stunning decision, a woman and her little girl were condemned to death without compassion in an act barely noticeable to an overburdened system and its weary workers.

Perhaps an unexpected legacy of the AIDS epidemic will be that we scrutinize health policy to learn when and how we disallowed human experience in the name of expediency. It is desperately important that we do.

The woman in New York, beyond her own brush with brutality, is a symbol—one welfare mother, one town, one disease, one situation. But like the Tomb of the Unknown Soldier, she embodies the heart of Everymother, everywhere, who knows no relief from the agony of despair in the face of disease, and who is granted no respite. Her solitude should be a sacred reminder to everyone, but especially to the public health advocate and the policy maker.

It is deeply important to understand the magnitude and the human dimension of this largely invisible issue. Otherwise, it is too easily dismissed in the myopia of economic jargon. It is not just AIDS or other catastrophic illness. It is not just welfare mothers. It is not just the inner city ghettos. A pressing global and universal spectrum must be understood, acknowledged, and internalized, if health policy is to reflect humanity. When we consider emotion and exhaustion, precious little difference exists between a mother of six in Appalachia and a first-time mother in Ann Arbor. Women's collective experience knows no demographic divides; it shares the unspoken truths of caring and caretaking, and part of that shared secret is the understanding that there is no relief.

An historical context bears on current reality. We should remember that the domain of healing traditionally rested with women. As midwives and healers throughout the ages, theirs was a tradition of sharing the knowledge and the burden of caretaking. Only in the Industrial Age, when health care became a commodity, were caring and curing rendered separate entities—with curing assigned to the male domain. By present day extension, and once again driven by economics, we see compassion further removed from caretaking and curing. It is no small coincidence that policy making remains largely in the hands of men, who may be more enlightened than their colleagues of the 19th century, but who have yet to stay home and rock the babies.

Where does this lead us, then, assuming a just society must act on its own enlightenment? Do we first legislate a more humane behavior? Do we seek from foundations and philanthropists houses filled with rocking chairs? Perhaps we begin by asking weary mothers who weep invisible tears.

But for God's sake, let us begin. And in the name of all that is decent, let us grant that mothers may once more rock their babies in their arms until they die.

There But For The Grace Of God

I stand at the counter waiting for the man to notice me. In the midst of the chaos around him, he is patient in the way that people devoid of expression and feeling are. When my turn comes, I explain that I am there to fill out papers so that my mother can remain in a nursing home. He is visibly relieved. In the realm of social service agency demands, this request is a piece of cake. He tells me that someone will be right with me.

I stand back to wait and watch. The room is typically barren and drab. The linoleum floor, which could use a wash and wax, is littered with old straw wrappers, crinkled Kleenex, a baby's pacifier. Plastic chairs ring the room, disinviting any social intercourse, making their occupants look like they are in a line-up. The silent string of people screams with body language. On the walls, a few stray posters admonish their audience on a variety of health practices; notices in fine print inform them of their rights.

At the far end of the room, an elderly woman bedecked in a cacophony of colored polyesters, argues heatedly in the most exquisite European accent with a young black man about whether or not it is appropriate to sit on a table. Despite looking silly, she sounds refined and eloquent, and is passionately committed to her position on the subject. "You laugh at me," she says in her Greta Garbo voice. "You think I'm not important. But tables are for putting nice things, not for sitting on!" The black man dances around her, taunting with a string of non sequiturs. "Yeah, Baby, we know. But maybe we ain't got no chairs. And 'sides, next week, I be 34 years old!" He saunters into the men's room singing, like the cock who won the fight. The woman sits down and talks to herself softly.

At the pay phone, a young woman looking increasingly impatient slumps against the black box. A cigarette dangles from her mouth. Her bleached hair is moussed into spikes which she fingers with red-painted nails that are probably false. The conversation appears to be one-sided, with only the rolling of her eyes for response.

Fifteen minutes have passed, so I ask the desk clerk if it will soon be my turn. "Didn't anyone come out yet?" he asks laconically. He picks up the phone and tells me again that someone will be with me shortly. This time I wait by the counter so he can't forget me.

Two women approach the counter, each with purple bruises on the left side of their faces. A sickening feeling creeps up my stomach. It seems unlikely that they've both had the same accident. More likely, they both know the same man.

At the Food Stamp counter, a sweet young woman clutching a baby whispers to the clerk, "Do you think I could get my Food Stamps today, instead of tomorrow?" Nearby, another young woman ignores her infant's wails, barking at her toddler, "James, git over here! Now set down! You behave yourself or I'm gonna spank your bottom!"

Next to me a Spanish social worker explains to a weary looking man with a mustache and two days' beard growth on his chin how to catch a bus to his destination. "Comprende?" she asks smiling. "Si," he says, but he makes no move. After a moment, she catches on. "Tiene dinero?" "No," he responds, looking down. Still smiling, she huddles with her colleagues, and when it appears that nothing official can be done, she disappears, returning with bus fare—no doubt from her own purse.

Finally, a young, bearded, liberal-looking worker emerges from the bowels of the bureaucracy and calls my name. He does a quick visual assessment, and appears relieved in a guarded sort of way. "I don't know how you handle this every day," I say (to let him know I'm not "one of them"). "Some days are worse than others," he says. We conclude our business, and he seems impressed that I write down his name—"just in case any problems arise," I explain.

He lets me out of the inner sanctum. It is close to 5:00 so the room is beginning to empty. Only a mother with her crying children and one of the bruised women remain. The clerk, still with the same frozen expression on his face, is pulling on his jacket, preparing to leave. In the evening light, the room is a barren wasteland, like the souls of the people who come there every day.

I get in my nice car, to drive to my big house where I will go on with my good life. No one will sign a paper so that I can eat. I will not have to come back here and answer private questions in a public place. I will be warm, much loved, and unharmed.

But I will be changed by the simple errand which took me on a journey across that deep chasm. I will remember. For I know that "there, but for the grace of God, go I."

No doubt, the Greta Garbo woman, and the soul-weary mother, and the woman with the bruised face, thought the very same thing when they looked at me.

VIGILANCE WITHOUT VENGEANCE

A nyone who has known me for longer than five minutes can attest to the fact that I am a card-carrying feminist. It is well known in local circles that with the reflexive instinct of an animal under attack, I will go to the mat with any man (or woman) on issues as far ranging as pay equity, paternalism, and pornography. So it hurts me to know that for what I am about to say, many a feminist will cry "Foul!" and even a friend or two will question my loyalty and my perspective, thinking of me at best as a temporary heretic, and at worst, as a sellout.

A colleague of mine, writing in a feminist periodical to which I also contribute, addressed an important issue—the co-optation of women-controlled health care by the male-dominated medical establishment. The fact that more and more hospitals promote their maternity services as "birth centers" and that increasingly, free-standing "women's health centers" are privately owned and operated by establishment physicians bears watching. It reflects a dangerous trend, with historical precedent, of men usurping the rhetoric of feminism for their own economic gain. Vigilance is certainly called for.

But when vigilance, on this or any other issue, becomes vengeful, we must question whether we are helping, or hurting. When, for example, former colleagues become the victim of a vendetta—suddenly in the "they" camp because they have taken a different approach on an issue than "we"—shouldn't we ask ourselves whether we are about to throw out the baby with the bath water? When we frame information for others in a way that is frightening and inciteful, potentially harmful in its lack of clarity or completeness, who are we serving?

More importantly, don't we need to stand back and question what our "mission" is as feminists? The question becomes even more significant when we are feminist journalists. I have always believed that, at least in part, our commitment is to validate and share information, the tools of empowerment when it comes to exercising our right to choice. When we begin to ask others to embrace dogma and ideology, in lieu of facilitating their own fact-finding because they have a right to know; when we sensationalize instead of inform; when we give partial information, because it builds our own case, or because there are still unanswered questions: have we not begun an act of disservice reminiscent of what we abhor in the mainstream?

I have been an involved feminist for many years now. In crucial ways, I owe perhaps not my life, but certainly my identity, to the movement, which I believe to be the most profound social phenomenon of our century. Feminists are family, and "for all thy faults, I love thee still." (A sentiment I take to be mutual.) But sometimes I look back, perhaps stimulated by something like my colleague's recent article, and from my perspective (possibly one of a little bit more age and experience?), I wonder where we are, and I worry about how far we seem not to have come. I listen to the dialogue between black and white women, disabled and able-bodied women, Jewish and non-Jewish feminists, moderates and radicals, feminists and "non-feminists," and realize how little has changed in a decade. I feel a kind of psychic fatigue that frightens me: so much to be done, so little time, so high a price for our own divisiveness.

If I am condemned by some sisters for this point of view (and it wouldn't be the first time), it certainly will hurt. But eventually I will get over it, because I know that feminist debate is at the heart of what we are all about; in many ways, it is the very source of our power.

So is our pluralism, our individuality, and our ability to approach problems and situations from a variety of perspectives. Once armed with information, and truly able to hear each other in all the variations of our "different voice," we are enriched immeasurably by the feminist range of possibility. Inherent in this belief is the notion of trust—not only among ourselves, but from others who look to us for critical thinking and support. When what we share with them is less than balanced and accurate, more weighted down in polemic than practical advice or proven fact, we let them down in serious and frightening ways.

Surely we, above all others, understand that to fail women like that is something against which we must be ever vigilant.

THE SECOND SEX, THE SECOND
GENERATION

S he bounces in the door, wide-eyed and animated, and ans-
wers the routine "How was your day?" with electric energy.
My sixteen-year-old daughter has just had her first class in
Feminist Literature.

"I can't believe it!" she says. "Only fifteen years ago
women couldn't get jobs and credit. I thought all that discrimination stuff was history. But it happened while I was alive!"

"Happened? What's with the past tense," I ask. "It's not
ancient history. It's here! It's now! It's us!"

It's my office colleague—senior, tenured, and female—who
has just learned that she will lose her secretarial support for
reasons of budget, while the new kid on the block—junior, less
well-credentialed, and male—is getting help so that he won't
have to do his own xeroxing.

It's NBC saying goodbye to a 39-year-old Jane Pauley, while
welcoming back a 64-year-old Joe Garagiola.

It's 19-year-old Gwen Dreyer dropping out of the U.S. Naval
Academy after being handcuffed by male midshipmen to a
urinal as part of hazing, while the men involved get a few
demerits and a weekend restriction.

It's a 17-year-old girl allegedly sexually assaulted in the back
of a limousine by members of a professional athletic team in the
nation's capital.

Discrimination, harassment, and sexism are hardly things of
the past. Fifteen, fifty, five hundred years later, they are
alive—and very, very sick.

Several years ago, I spent a good deal of time lecturing on
college campuses, and I could see it then: this idea among
young women that we had done it. The "army" of the 1960's,

they thought, had wiped out the scourge of anti-woman sentiment, and now they could simply get on with their corporate, upwardly mobile, have-it-all lives. How wrong, how terribly wrong they were.

Like those who say "it could never happen again" while Jewish cemeteries are being desecrated and swastikas appear on synagogues (and I realize the limitations of the comparison), any woman who thinks "it's over" either is working overtime at denial or just hasn't looked left and right in a long time. This kind of complacency isn't just irritating and perhaps selfish; it's dangerous. Because what happens to each one of us is the mirror of our mutual fate, even if we are not directly victimized.

A feminist once said that to be a misogynist a man must hate women and to be a chauvinist, he must fear them. To Gwen Dreyer and to my friend, to Jane Pauley and to a violated 17-year-old, and indeed to all of us, the distinction is moot.

The important message to our daughters is to be alert not so much to definitions as to deeds—those daily occurrences by which we measure progress and the potential of our collective future. For this, history is indeed prologue, and viewed from that perspective, we would do well to reflect on the words of Lady Grove, writing in *The Human Woman* in 1908: "To speak of the (woman's) movement as a transitory wave already on the decline seems due to an extraordinary inability to grasp the goal towards which the human race is inevitably creeping."

The time line and the milestones by which we measure the attainment of that goal rests in large part with our daughters. Judging from the reaction of mine at this early stage of her awakening, I am encouraged. After all, today was only her first class, and already her peripheral vision seems markedly improved.

POWER WOMEN, WOMAN POWER

Something is wrong in the heartland of Feminism. I know, because after nearly 20 years of living there, I shouldn't feel like a stranger in my own land. I shouldn't feel like a tourist, a voyeur, a charlatan when I have been invited to join a group of prominent women in welcoming 25 Soviet women to America. Yet, despite the fact that my name tag was there with the best of them, that is exactly how I felt as I rode up the elevator to the penthouse atrium of one of Washington's most prestigious office buildings not long ago.

I made my way through the sea of faces, looking for someone—anyone—who would smile at me, but no one did, not even the women who have seen me at similar functions for years. Eventually I found one of the organizers of the event that this cocktail party was initiating, and introduced myself, explaining that as a journalist, I wanted to cover the historic meeting. She was momentarily impressed, but suddenly, mid-sentence, she squealed, "Oh my God, there's Coretta!" and with lightning speed abandoned me for the notable Mrs. King.

I stood there, mouth open. "How extraordinary!" I said to the woman next to me, who had seen the transaction.

"Washington," she replied knowingly. Later, as I was leaving, she gave me her card—an act of great friendship and camaraderie. I was touched, and we agreed, laughingly, to "do lunch" one of these days.

The whole three days were like that. I observed, I participated, I felt like an outsider.

By the end of the meeting, I had befriended three Russians and offended one American—the co-convener, who had no idea who I was despite the fact that we have been conferencing together since circa 1978. How can it be, I mused, that I know her name and where she comes from, and the most she can say of me is that I have "a familiar face." When I offered, as a feminist journalist, to become more involved with her organization, she said that would be terrific, but while I was digging out my card, she wandered off with a Big Name from a Big Organization. And that is when I offended her. "Elizabeth!" I called out, hand on my hip. "Do you want my card or do you not?" She was embarrassed; I was enraged.

There is something wrong in the heartland of Feminism, and those three days reminded me of what it is, and why I am a stranger in my own land.

What is wrong is that for all our polemic about power, that most corrupting of male traits, we also embrace it, play games with it, abuse it, use it. Like our male counterparts, we like it—so much that even in the midst of our ideology and our rhetoric we hurt others with it.

Judith Plant, writing in the preface to *Healing the Wounds*, says something that helps me understand that dynamic as it is played out here and elsewhere. "There is no respect for the 'other' in patriarchal society. The other. . . . is considered only insofar as it can benefit the subject. So self-centered is this view that it is blind to the fact that its own life depends on the integrity and well-being of the whole." Plant writes in the context of environmental preservation and integrity, but her message is far-reaching. She advocates for change, not only outside of ourselves, but inside as well, and asks for a transformation of power, "as the discovery of our own strength."

Ironically, that is the very message that this convocation of women would bring to the world's power brokers. The problem is that while dealing with the macro level of domination and oppression, the micro level of one's own behavior gets short shrift. The feminist vision, it would seem, has an astigmatism.

There is something of a post script to this point of view. On the same weekend that the above scene was played out, I also had the opportunity to meet and spend time with the women of the House of Ruth, one of Washington's women's shelters. I had gone, for the first time, as a volunteer. None of these women had ever seen me before. They had every reason to suspect my motives in being there. It was clear that I could not know first-hand anything of their experience; yet, I was treated with courtesy and interest. In the one and a half hours that I spent with these women and their babies, we did some real talking. We began to get acquainted. Genuine and healthy curiosity flowed between us. Questions got honest answers, and asking caused no embarrassment. I look forward to going back next month, and I think they'll be glad to see me too. Those are some strong women, capable and coping, against all kinds of odds.

I am indebted to the women of the House of Ruth. They showed me the difference between powerful women and the power of women, and reminded me once more why I'm a feminist.

It was a gift Judith Plant might have called a healing experience.

Apocalypse Now

Y ou detect it in their faces, taut and lined. You hear it in their lowered voices. Most of all you see it in their eyes, darting or downcast, intense and searching. Women are frightened. Deeply, darkly frightened.

Sometimes, when it feels safe, they seek you out to talk about it. Other times the fear is buried behind symbolic issues—panic, for example, at the imminence of losing a job ill-conceived in the first place, or a marriage failing because her husband wants to run away from home just as it's time to finance their children's college educations. Maybe she's a young mother who doesn't quite know why she feels so lethargic and despondent. She could be a welfare mother who knows exactly why she feels that way but still has to feed her kids today. She could be urban or rural, rich or poor, black or white, American or Asian. But she is realizing a growing terror.

Why is she so afraid? I believe it is because in some essential corner of her being she knows that things are out of control in a very big way. She knows intuitively that there is mounting cosmic chaos, and that we are heading for what the Navajo Indians call a "box canyon," a place where we will be trapped by a nameless, faceless enemy who has lived among us for a very long time and whom we have been powerless to remove. It is this powerlessness that she internalizes, this knowing that something is deeply wrong in the fabric of humanity, that finds its way out of her in anxiety and depression, and free-floating fear.

She knows that increasingly things don't make sense and that there is less and less room for a moral imperative and value-based living. She understands with chilling clarity that we are out of control and that the world's priorities are incredibly and dangerously crazy. She believes that in the not very distant future we will all pay a terrible price for this reality.

This perspective is not esoteric: it is born out by everything we see around us. We all know that the numbers of homeless are growing, that our children are being raised into illiteracy and disease, that AIDS and breast cancer and substance abuse are epidemics unattended in rational proportion, and that the earth is what E.L. Doctorow has described as "shriveling into a kind of radioactive ember." Our so-called leadership obsesses over removing the rights of privacy from women, or limiting artistic expression, but ignores social problems of such enormous magnitude that to see them firsthand is to turn away or to weep. Defense expenditures in the U.S. are larger than the gross national products of all but eight countries in the world. The so-called entertainment industry invests and recoups growing millions of dollars on sex and violence. Anti-semitism, racism, sexism, and other forms of heinous discrimination are visibly on the rise. It is even becoming hip and mainstream to display one's hatred, misogyny, and ethnocentrism—just ask Jimmy Breslin.

Think about this in a global context. Why are ethnic pogroms on the rise? How is it that fetuses are aborted simply on the grounds of gender, or that women are still burned in the name of dowry? Why, when we know that 75 percent of illnesses in developing countries are caused by unsafe water and inadequate sanitation, don't we clean up the water? (The estimated cost to do this is $20 billion, less than two weeks of the world's expenditures on armaments.) Why do we not value the ecosystem when we know what is happening to our planet? When we know the facts about Chernobyl, why do we persist in promoting nuclear energy? As Marilyn Waring says in her powerful and urgent book *If Women Counted: A New Feminist Economics*, "This is not a sane state of affairs. What is the origin of such madness?"

Women may not be able to fully answer that question, but they have a terrifying vision of its implications for the world and for the legacy towards which we are hurtling our children.

They feel palpably what writers like Vaclav Havel, poet and president of Czechoslovakia, and E.L. Doctorow have tried to bring to human consciousness: "the terrible universal darkness around us, and the tragedy of death." They search for compassion, common sense, honesty, and a just civilization, but are continually thwarted by the world's dysfunctional and corrupt political, economic, and social institutions.

That hope eludes them—as did a different title and closing for this essay—is in itself frightening. Perhaps one day, before it's too late, we will all find room for revision.

LEARNING TO LIVE WITH THE "F" WORD

One of the sadder legacies of the 1988 presidential campaign, you will recall, was the contamination of the word "liberal." In a stunning public relations coup, the right wing managed to make credible the notion that humanism was a dangerous and subversive thing, something to be avoided at all costs. Standing in the wings as the beleaguered Democratic candidate turned one cheek and then the other, the silent majority begged, unheard, for the "L" word to be worn, shouted, whispered, emblazoned on his lapel like a veritable Red Badge of Courage. Take pride! Tell them what it really means! we wanted to cry out, but none of us did, outside of our private conversations with the already converted.

There is always a lesson to be learned, of course, and the lesson of the "L" word needs to be embraced by women, and men, who call themselves feminists—and those who carefully do not.

I have heard just once too often recently a disturbing caveat, the proud preemptive: "I'm not a feminist, but . . . " As in "I'm not a feminist, but I believe in equal pay for equal work"; "I'm not a feminist, but I certainly can take care of myself!"; "I'm not a feminist, but I expect to be able to make my own decisions about whether or not to have children." And so on.

We need to understand that "feminist" is not a dirty word. It does not necessarily nor always stand for militancy, separatism, Marxist polemic, or sexual preferences that are different from our own. Even in those cases where that may be part of the package, the common denominator defines us as feminists; that denominator is the basic and profound belief that no

individual or system has the right to inhibit another, to reduce
its freedom, or to limit its potential.

This lesson was powerfully illustrated some years ago in
Utah. Researchers on a door-to-door survey asked, "Do you
agree with the ERA?" "Oh, no!" was the resounding reply,
some 94 percent of the time. However, when the exact language of the Equal Rights Amendment was read to the same
people, and they were asked if they agreed with the statement,
98 percent said yes. Nowhere in its text, they were astonished
to see, did the ERA remotely suggest that men and women
would be forced to use the same public toilets. (And while
we're setting the record straight, no feminist is known to ever
have burnt her bra publicly. That non-event was the invention
of an overzealous journalist with a penchant for fantasy.)

We need to understand the importance of owning the word
"feminist," because of the backlash that occurs out of our
refusal to do so. As an example, let us remember the reporting
of the massacre of women students at a Montreal university.
The first reports said that the gunman had gone looking for
"FEMinists," that "FEMinists" were perceived by him as
responsible for his problems, even that "FEMinists" may well
have brought on the attack by their recent "No Means No"
campaign against date rape. Reporters practically spit the word
out, as if, somehow, it began to explain the perversity behind
the atrocity. How curious that when women were shot, they
were referred to as feminists, and yet when feminists make a
political statement or take a "non-political" position, the press
cautiously avoids using that term, as if to do so would be to give
legitimacy to their concerns.

We—and they—have got it all backwards, and we need desperately, and quickly, to set the record straight. It is no exaggeration to say that the fate of all of us rests in the balance.

"What's in a name?" Shakespeare once asked. Perhaps the
answer, for liberals and for feminists, is nothing more and
nothing less than the truth of who we are.

YOM KIPPUR

It's the same every year at Yom Kippur.

Slipping further away from the rituals binding me to a Jewish childhood, I wonder about the relevance of attending a service, the words of which, if truth be told, hold little inherent personal meaning for me. I toy with the idea of not joining the temple-less congregation which assembles only annually. But something continues to draw me, something more than habit. Perhaps it is the safety of anchoring in tradition. Maybe it's guilt. Whatever the motivation, my Jewish identity emerges, predictably pulling me towards the Kol Nidre, year after year.

And year after year, it's the same. I enter the "temple," which for this itinerant congregation is the ecumenical chapel of a progressive Unitarian Church, find a place, open a prayer book. At the first responsive reading, my eyes cloud over. At the beloved prayer, "And thou shalt love the Lord thy God with all thy heart . . . ," the tears spill. At the singing of the Kol Nidre—last year with the pure soprano voice of a female cantor—I feel I shall weep uncontrollably.

It is because it's the same every year at Yom Kippur.

At once, I am bound to every Jew in every place and at every time. As far as I can reach side to side in my imagination a Jew stands beside me, moved also by the eternal chant. In California, in Kracow, in Belgium and Bulgaria, in Russia and Romania, in Europe, Africa, Asia—in every corner of the globe, a Jew is standing, swaying, weeping, praying with me. And as far forward as I can think, and as far backward as I can remember, a Jew is also at my side. I share this Kol Nidre with the Jews of the Warsaw Ghetto, and the Jews of the camps. I share it with the Jews who prayed in fear during the pogroms, and the Jews who will petition to leave the Soviet Union. I stand beside the Jews who pioneered in Israel, and the American West, and the European frontiers. I am on Hester Street, and in the factories, and in the Williamsburg ghetto, and with George Gershwin and Fanny Brice, and with the unnamed girls who died in the factory fire of New York. I am suddenly everywhere and in every time in which there is a Jew to remember and to reach out to. I am standing next to my Uncle Leo in his beloved temple in Toronto, and I see my father long ago in the tiny synagogue of my childhood. I see the children of my children and the progeny of all Judaism. A million lifetimes flash before me, and bind me forever to Jewish being. And then I understand why I always come back.

It was like this last year, and it will be like this next year. It's the same every year at Yom Kippur.

AUTUMN REFLECTIONS

When I was a child, I hated autumn, its night darkness closing in on me like an odd juxtaposition of reality and metaphor.

Much later, I grew to love it, with its cool, crisp air full of promise and energy, its vibrant colors a nature rainbow.

Today is a quiet Saturday in early October, the air cool and crisp. Tree colors tumble out of a canvas that begins with primary blues and greens. But once again I feel like a child. Sadness overwhelms me like a humid twilight.

Today, on the Mall in front of the nation's capitol, people marched for housing. Weary, hungry, sad, numbed people, pleading for something so basic as a roof over their heads. Nearby, acres and acres of AIDS quilt wept to us of lost lives. Not very far away, the Vietnam Wall wept too.

Last night, I had dinner with people I call friends. I heard them utter, with total conviction, every myth of poverty, and each oath of the "Me" Generation. They think the hungry babies, the crack babies, the AIDS babies have nothing to do with them.

Today, in shopping malls all across the country, people will carry on as usual. They will stroll, savor, and spend. While they do, thousands of children around the world will die for lack of immunization and clean water, and some of them will even be in this country, but nobody will know their names or faces and so it will have nothing to do with them. Nor will the accidental shootings by Saturday night specials, nor the environmental pollution creeping over this good earth, nor the corruption in high places, nor the apathy that hurtles us toward the winter of our discontent.

Tell me, on this crisp, cool, colorful autumn day: how shall I keep the terror of night away?

You Gotta' Love It

~

WEEKEND IN LA LA LAND

A lice in Wonderland, wrote Martin Gardner in *The Annotated Alice*, was the jest of Lewis Carroll, his way of poking fun at the "monstrous mindlessness of the cosmos." Well, the kind Mr. Carroll (a.k.a. Reverend C.L. Dodgson) may have been laughing, but others of us find it rather difficult on occasion. Take my recent weekend during which I came perilously close to following the rabbit into that deep dark hole.

It began on a Friday in the place where I spend a good many of my working hours, a business firm of high repute. We have been told that the project to which I dedicate my time happens to have something of a temporary cash flow problem. The client has been a bit slow in forking over the finances, it seems, and we are now each "free to find some billable time elsewhere this year." Why this situation has occurred is open to various interpretations, but the bottom line is we're broke. So I have a very hard time understanding my boss, who begins to sound like the mad hatter when he calls several of us into his office with this announcement: "I want to run a workshop! It will be a good thing for us and it won't cost much."

"As in the low zeros?" I ask, having just started to process the last piece of news.

He laughs politely, and proceeds to lay out the plans for an extravagant event that will take place in another country, adding travel and hotel to the mounting costs of this growing fantasy. Sheepishly, I counsel against such a seminar just now, but am contained by two enthusiastic colleagues. Sounding suddenly like Tweedledum and Tweedledee, they make a case for what they euphemistically refer to as a "great opportunity." I smile and back out of the room, thinking that I am missing something which will no doubt become clear as I am recycling paper clips in the name of austerity. Tea, anyone?

On my way home, I run a few errands that leave me feeling "curiouser and curiouser." At the grocery store, for example, a woman asks me to break a dozen eggs in half for her. "I'm always ripping up the boxes," she explains. The dairy man, busy stocking shelves, overhears this exchange and races toward us.

"That's why we've got these new boxes!" he beams, thrusting a carton of eight eggs in her hand. "Trying to cut down on everyone breaking up the boxes."

I cannot resist. "But if people continue to want six eggs, why do you package them in eights?"

"To stop 'em breaking the boxes," he says, looking at me like I'm not getting the point.

"Wouldn't it be more sensible to put them in boxes of six?"

"We're trying to help," he assures me patiently. "That's why we've got these new boxes." He points again to the newly stacked cartons of eight, and I slink away. Oh dear, as Alice said, how puzzling it all is.

At the pharmacy, I decide to wait for my son's prescription, which involves nothing more than pulling three packets off the shelf and typing a label. "That will be twenty minutes," the clerk says without looking up.

"Excuse me," I say. "Why would that be?"

"We have all these other people in front of you."

I look around. There is absolutely no one else at, or near, the counter. I point this out.

"There are other people ahead of you!" the clerk snaps.

"But none of them is here waiting for their label to be typed," I plead. The pharmacist, who has overheard this exchange, shoots me a glance somewhere between hostile and enraged, and begins to peck at my label. Doesn't pharmacy school include Typing 101 yet? "Faster, faster!" as the Queen said.

The looking glass world continues as later that evening we

decide to take in a movie for relaxation. We arrive late so I ask the usher how much of the feature film we have missed.

"The movie started 15 minutes ago."

"Yes, but how much of the feature have we missed?"

"Fifteen minutes."

"Have we missed 15 minutes of the FEATURE?"

"The movie started 15 minutes ago." Jabberwocky.

Laughter, Reinhold Niebuhr said, is a kind of no man's land between faith and despair. Lewis Carroll found that space with Alice. Others less fortunate, like myself, continue to search for it, "down, down, down," wondering all the while, as Alice did, "Will the fall never come to an end?" The difference between us and Alice, of course, is that frightening as it may seem, we are already awake. "What a curious feeling" indeed.

CODE BLUE, OR CAN THIS EMERGENCY ROOM BE SAVED?

M y son's earache had started quietly enough—an after school non-event. Medicated by seven and sleeping peacefully by nine, he seemed fine. When he awoke at midnight, crying and writhing, we were alarmed—knowing full well that when a 12-year-old boy asks to be taken to the hospital for pain relief, it is not a request to be ignored. Jumping into our jeans, we braced ourselves for The Emergency Room Experience, which we had not been through for several years, and on which occasion the word "incompetence" took on a whole new meaning.

Things seemed relatively quiet as we checked in with Admissions. The clerk, a large, calm woman, was the kind whose bosom you can imagine wanting to sink into as you sign away your valuables and your dignity. She smiled as she keypunched our particulars. "Religion?"

"Half and half," we said. "Maybe you could put 'J/C'."

"We don't have a code for that," she laughed. In the end, she entered "Hebrew," which seemed, at least historically, to cover all the bases.

All at once, a commotion from behind the double doors made its way past us.

"Come on, John," a nurse cajoled. "You can't leave until the doctor sees you. Be reasonable now."

John seemed ambivalent and confused as he allowed himself to be led back into the inner sanctum.

The Admissions lady clicked away at the copious paperwork without batting an eye. Entering our phone number for the third time from memory, she said, like a twinkling Mrs. Santa Claus, "I'm an Oldie but Goodie!"

Finally another nurse called us back. Assigning us a cubby, she checked vital signs, assuring us that "someone will be with you in just a moment." The phrase had the distinct ring of "the check is in the mail."

Next to us was a young woman who, it seems, had managed to dislocate her shoulder in vigorous foreplay (Ah, Youth!). Opposite, a man with what must have been a broken nose lay quietly, bandages pressing his face flat. There were a few others looking innocuously unwell (one of whom turned out to be an attending physician), but nothing of high drama.

Meanwhile, John grew ever more agitated. Stalking the area, he began spewing obscenities, most of which began with the four-letter "F" word.

"Stay in your room, John!" ordered the nurse. "This is a hospital. You have to respect people's privacy."

This was, of course, ridiculous. Each patient's "room" consisted of flimsy curtains—ensuring that every grunt, groan, and confidence was in the public domain. Furthermore, at no point in the entire track of curtain was there enough fabric for ends to meet. A sea of people to-ing and fro-ing had full access to General Hospital's Classic Peep Show, if they were so inclined.

As it turned out, the entourage was soon to include hospital security and eventually, the County Police. John was becoming more violent, and more verbally abusive.

"He's a real shit, isn't he?" said a young nurse with long pink fingernails and a lot of make-up to an officious guy in surgical greens who later turned out to be an orderly with an ego problem. The remark, and her appearance, stunned me. Years ago, in what seems like another incarnation, I had been a nursing student. At that time, the nursing profession was still kissing cousins with the militant matrons and sisters of the British system. Rigid rules included short, unpolished nails, clean, white-only uniforms, no hair touching collars, deference to docs, and of course, silence, obedience, and modesty. Now, I'm certainly not a proponent of the physicians' handmaiden myth. But really, is that any way for a nice nurse to talk?

By now it was after 1:00 a.m., and my home remedies of aspirin, ear drops, and ice packs had begun to work. When the tall, dark, and handsome Dr. Kildare-type walked in, my son was calmly dozing on the trolley (despite John's histrionics). Peering into the painful ear, the young doctor immediately suggested a different antibiotic than what the pediatrician had prescribed only hours earlier. "It costs about 80 bucks," he said, "but it works well."

"Why don't we see if the other stuff works first?" I suggested.

"Okay. I'm just going to the station for another instrument."

I don't know quite where "the station" was, but it seemed to be rather a long trip. About half an hour later, he returned. After a good look at the "whopper of an infection," he suggested a painkiller. "That's really what we came in for," I reminded him meekly. (Old habits die hard.)

Once again, he disappeared. Broken Nose, Dislocated Shoulder, and Earache waited some more. John, in the meantime, was becoming rather frightening. "Where are the cops? Call 911!" said the manicured nurse.

The police showed up and somehow must have restrained John, who grew ominously quiet; the police officers huddled at the nurses' station reviewing their legal options. Their presence was comforting, unlike their state of confusion about what could be done. At one point Mrs. Claus passed by. "Could you let my husband know that we're all right?" I asked her. "If he's aware of all this commotion, he might be worried."

"I'll only mention it if he seems concerned," she winked.

About 2:00 a.m., Dr. Kildare returned but seemed in no hurry to discharge anyone. At the desk, a gaggle of nurses, doctors, police, and security guards reviewed the John drama.

"Anyone have change for a five?" asked Kildare. "I need some M&Ms." Catching my glance, he added, "I'll have you outta here in just a minute!"

Finally, a prescription, "Emergency Room Instructions," and

two Tylenol-with-Codeine were presented to us. Our name
was erased from the board, along with Dislocated Shoulder.
(Broken Nose had to stay. Perhaps he had sustained a concus-
sion?) As we left, Dr. Kildare and Mrs. Santa Claus said
goodbye. John screamed out, "F— you!"

When we got home, we gave our son one of the painkillers
and tucked him in.

I hoarded the other one, hoping he wouldn't need it before
morning. I thought it might come in handy for the world-class
headache I was harboring, as I slipped into sleep, the clock
glowing 3:00.

THE CATALOG CULTURE

It all began when a colleague of mine left the country long term. She had her mail forwarded to the office, to be sent in regular weekly dispatches to her new location in the African bush. Weekly, as her mail packet was being assembled, great "oohs" and "aahs" emanated from the mail room, along with managerial groans about the weight (and therefore the cost) of her correspondence.

"What's it all about?" I asked the secretary one day.

"It's all that luscious mail order stuff," she replied. "She's a regular catalog queen!"

Against my better judgment, I decided to peruse the goodies. There in a plethora of pages full of color and couture was every conceivable piece of fashion, footwear, kitchen gadgetry, garden accoutrement, camping supply, and recreational adjunct you could ever dream of (as well as some you wouldn't have thought up in a million years). The catalogs, it turned out, were well shared with the office staff before being bundled up—somewhat the worse for wear—and sent to their original addressee.

Now, as I had discovered this phenomenon, it seemed only appropriate that I should be included in the routing of these catalogs, for a quick look-see. I conned myself that it was better than pausing for a cup of coffee, and a lot more healthy—as long as I didn't put pen to paper.

Which, inevitably, of course I did.

Only once, you understand, but that was enough. Send back one teensy-weensy little post card requesting one itsy-bitsy little complimentary catalog, and I can assure you that within one calendar year, you will be on every mailing list of every mail order house in the entire country.

What's worse is that if you are anything like me, you will not be able to resist placing just one itty-bitty little order, probably at Christmastime, and from that time on, you will be hooked. Addicted. An habitual user. A lifetime lover of the flipped page, do-it-in-the-privacy-of-your-own-home, call now pay later, shopping set. Your best friends will forever be named such dependables as L.L. Bean, J. Crew, Eddie Bauer, Lillian Vernon, Land's End. Like a soap opera buff, you will call your other friends to share the latest.

"Have you SEEN what Eddie's out with?"

"No, but Lillian sure hasn't been up to very much lately, has she?"

"Well, I don't know about that, but J. and L.L. certainly haven't let any grass grow under their feet! Have you seen that fabulous flannel lounging robe?"

The Fraternal (or Sororal) Order of Catalog Lovers, it turns out, is quite an extensive, if not exclusive, group: largely due to our increasingly mobile lifestyles, it would appear that the subculture is now a global one. I can regularly count on receiving at least one international offering per high season, and I have taken to trading tips and bargains with friends from afar. It goes something like this: "If you get me two jumpers from that Scottish woolen mill, and I send you the long johns from Land's End, we should be just about even, right?"

I don't even try to talk myself out of it anymore. After all, who can resist the purring camaraderie of that anonymous telephone friend, ever available night and day, seven days a week, who knows everything about you from your favorite color to your inseam; and who never, never gets cross no matter how many items you return.

Still, there may come a time when it has really gone too far, and those of us thoroughly dependent on paginated picture mail have to fess up and cut down. If that day comes, I hope there's a Catalog Consumers Anonymous support group. I don't think I could go cold turkey.

Which reminds me, have you SEEN that marvelous little gourmet book with all the miniature baking pans in the shape of fish and veggies? Do you suppose if I got you one of those, you could send me. . . .

And How Was Your Day?

The first thing to be said about what follows is that I am not making this up (as side-splitting humorist Dave Barry is wont to say). What I am about to tell you really happened to me today. Why I am telling you has to do with catharsis and compassion. As we all know, misery loves company; and things could always be worse. I thought it just might be useful to clip this column and tuck it away in your wallet or glove compartment, for that rainy day when Murphy's Law takes over YOUR life.

Ironically, my Ultimate Bad Day began with a good deal of promise. Crisp and autumnal, it suggested efficiency, and I set about my tasks with uncharacteristic vigor. I should have known better, of course, since my first stop was the post office—a guaranteed downer, as we all know.

The circumstances of my visit were an irritant to begin with. Not one, but two postal errors had necessitated my return to my local branch office, where each clerk has passed courses in Surly 101 and The Art of Getting Things Done in Two Easy Speeds—Slow and Dead. The greater of my two concerns had to do with $15 worth of International Reply Coupons (IRCs)—a form of prepaid postage for overseas mail—which are only valid if stamped by the U.S. postal system. I had realized after a recent purchase that mine were not stamped, which I explained to the clerk.

"Receipt?" she snapped.

"I have lots of post office receipts," I said, growing testy, "but none of them say IRCs!"

"How do I know where you got these then? You could have found them on the street. Nothing I can do. Next!"

"Just a moment," I screeched. "That is totally unacceptable!

I have $15 worth of these things, and they're useless because of a post office error. Get me your supervisor!"

In the end, having been cheered on by the man next in line, my IRC's were stamped. Triumphant, I moved on, rewarding myself with a cup of take-out coffee from the local deli.

I was just beginning to feel restored, enjoying the leafy scenery of fall as I drove to my next stop, when the boulder hit my windshield. That the glass stayed intact while I did not was probably predictable. Not that I did anything foolish or over-reactive. Jumping out of my seat was a purely reflexive act, and it was inevitable that the very hot coffee I had just purchased nearly scalded me as it stained my clothes in erratic patterns of beige. "——!" I exclaimed. Nevertheless, I kept my wits about me (Kipling would have been proud), pulling into a garden nursery to dry out and regroup.

This act of control, as it happened, appeared the perfect opportunity to a swarm of killer bees who dove into my sunroof with kamikaze vengeance. No doubt I looked like Laurel and Hardy viewed on "fast forward" as I tried furiously to extricate myself, swatting at what must have seemed invisible demons to anyone watching the charade.

I regained my composure reasonably well. Deciding not to go home for a change of clothes, I proceeded on my way—smack into a fender-bending pile-up caused by a motorist whose yellowing driver's license was probably dated circa 1925. The good news is that I didn't actually hit anything myself, render-ing me quite free to move on to further petty disasters.

Nothing earth shattering, you realize, but the sort of thing that drives one slowly, surely, and invisibly twitchy. Like going to pick up the pictures of your vacation—six rolls of irreplace-able posterity—and being told that they're lost. ("But if we find them, they're free!") Or pulling up to the automatic bank teller to be told by a blinking computer sign, "Sorry, out of order. Try again later!" Or reaching home with every fiber of your being screaming "defeat" to find not a single tea bag in the entire house when all that you could think of to soothe you on the way there was a cup o'tea.

Sure, things could always be worse; tomorrow's a new day, and all the rest of it. But from where I sit as I write this, which is perilously close to curled up in the fetal position sucking my thumb, you'd have a hard time convincing me of that just now.

DOES IT RING TRUE?

M ost of us are now used to being assaulted, benevolently of course, by the U.S. Postal Service's daily delivery of junk mail. We have learned to deal with the intrusion and insult, which constitutes 90 percent of my mailbox contents, by trashing the mounds of officious-looking paper after visual scrutiny. My own rule of thumb is that anything that arrives with a window address, a sort-code, or "Occupant/Family/ Resident" is an immediate circular file.

But brave is the soul that can let a telephone go unanswered. Maybe I was conditioned in the 1950's and 1960's when young women sat by the phone waiting for someone—anyone—to call. Whatever the reason, I simply must answer the ring. Lately, however, I have been deluged by syrupy strangers who think that, in the name of American entrepreneurial spirit, they can invade my privacy carte blanche. I have raced to relieve the ringing more times than I care to count only to be solicited by representatives of every kind of service from lawns to funerals. These calls occur with disturbing regularity at the dinner hour; but recently, I suffered the penultimate intrusion. I was awakened before 9:00 a.m. on a Saturday by someone actually selling good will in the form of a foreign student exchange program. Normally I would be only too happy to open my arms to a visitor. On this occasion I'm afraid what I opened was my mouth, and I'm pretty sure it cost that well-intentioned program an articulate volunteer.

Even the *New York Times* has stooped to such tactics. To make matters worse, it proved to be infuriatingly inefficient and persisted with call-backs long after I had requested that my name be deleted from the invisible and powerful list that seems to have gotten into the hands of marketers everywhere.

Will it never end? I've thought about everything from going

unlisted to ripping the phone out of the wall. I even considered begging my Congresswoman, in the name of human decency, to propose legislation that would mandate intruders to cease and desist. This seemed viable, but my optimism was short lived. Before I could reach for the phone, the Democratic National Committee was on the line asking for a contribution.

"She moved!" I snapped. "And she didn't leave a forwarding phone number!"

I GAVE AT THE RED LIGHT

This time the fine art of fund raising has gone too far. I mean, I'm all for saving whales, cleaning up the environment, and fighting plagues and pestilence. But must I, in the already punishing course of "schlepping" kids around every Saturday, be accosted in the sanctity of my car?

A recent Saturday is the case in point. In an unusually brutal day of dentists, doctors, and dance lessons, I scurried around the parameters of my community like a self-impressed cockroach. Frozen in the driver mode (which is only one step removed from the fetal position), I carried out my duties in stoic—if slightly catatonic—fashion. My one solace as I embarked on these missions of motherhood was that no one could reach me by phone. What I hadn't bargained for, however, was the bevy of bright teenagers stationed at every traffic light, tin can in hand. No sooner had the green switched to amber than these agile figures, darting in and out, began knocking on car windows. "Give to Kids With Cancer!" they shouted. Next ensued mad attempts to reach for purses and wallets before the green. After all, it was one thing to be caught stingy, but supposing one of these altruistic collectors got run over just because we hadn't been willing to give fast enough?

Whoever dreamed this up makes direct mail marketing look like child's play.

Fact is, I can remember a time when only letters from people we knew arrived by post. They were never addressed to "Current Occupant," or "Sort Code CLI 123." Telephone calls were actually from someone whose voice had a familiar face. People asked "how are you tonight?" because they really cared. It would have been unheard of "in those days" for syrupy strangers to invade the dinner hour in the name of everything from gun control to great books.

When someone rang your doorbell, depending on the time of day, it was likely to be the baker, a neighbor, or your father. On the odd occasion that an itinerant junkman or traveling salesman came around, it was cause for curiosity and excitement. Today, five will get you ten that somebody is flogging something.

Even when the causes are commendable, it wears thin. Especially when they're three deep. Not long ago, I answered a dinnertime doorbell to find a menagerie, palms outstretched.

"Evening, Ma'am," said the first in line, a slender man whose jacket had the Rescue Squad emblem prominently placed. "Care to contribute?"

As I wrote out a check, I said to the little girl behind him, "Helping your dad out tonight?"

"No, but do you want to buy some Girl Scout Cookies?"

"Oh. And I suppose the little guy behind you is selling candy."

"Hey! How'd you know?" asked the beaming junior salesman, pressing a brochure in my hand explaining his mission.

Is there no end in sight? The mania already stretches from the mail to the malls, from the workplace to worship houses, from friend to friend, and stranger to stranger. Will no place be sacrosanct when it comes to solicitation? I suppose one of these days public lavatories will provide for philanthropic opportunities. Restaurants may start revolving funds. Train and airplane passengers may find themselves pleasantly pressed by uniformed aisle urchins.

If that day ever comes, I have a ready reply. You see, "I gave at the red light."

FORGIVE ME SEAT 12-B, FOR
I HAVE SINNED

On a recent trans-Atlantic flight, fate and the computer placed me next to an attractive middle-aged businessman of some prominence. By the time we left the coast of New-foundland, I was fully versed in the details of his marital crisis. When we reached the point-of-no-return, I understood his career conflicts, and as we touched down in London I was fully conversant with the challenges of rearing his two teenage children.

Airplanes have become today's confessional-cum-psychiatrist couch, for reasons which are easily understood. In such a fast-paced and highly stressful world, we all need the ear of a therapist or priest now and again. What better way than to seek the solace we crave from a complete stranger—someone for whom we will always be anonymous, and from whom we can flee when we have revealed more than intended. Rarely will we receive such undivided attention, or have the opportunity to extend the traditional 50-minute hour to such lengths—and at no additional cost!

Perhaps this phenomenon occurs more frequently in those of us who are less than comfortable about flying. Tap one anxiety and you tap them all. Or maybe it is the more burdened among us, or the more verbal. No doubt a scientific study, or content analysis, would unmask amazing data for both church and state. But for those of us with a less analytical bent, the bonding is sufficient unto itself. Nothing is more comforting than to share, over a scotch-and-water, the guilt one feels over childrearing, or the rage at one's boss, or the knowledge that you have let a best friend down. Miraculously, people who might otherwise strike us as callow and unfeeling

become masters of active listening—as if some correlation exists
between altitude and empathy, we find ourselves accepted and
acknowledged by these brave new partners. They understand
at once our morals and our motives. They forgive us our
trespasses and our neuroses. And then, like little angels and
phantom Freuds, they disappear out of our lives carrying our
trusted secrets into infinity.

Occasionally, of course, it doesn't work that way. We find
ourselves instead seated next to someone diabolically opposed
to our own value system—the devil incarnate, or a behaviorist
type. Worse still is the seat mate whose sole communication
consists of a sideways glance that conveys emphatically an
unwillingness to converse. We might assume in these cases
that we are sharing airborne space with someone who operates
at the level of perpetual moral sin or persistent pathology, in
which case it is best to ask the flight attendant to find a more
congenial seat.

More often than not, though, the law of the six mile high
Confessional and Couch Club holds up, serving us frequent
flyers well. So next time you're traveling for business or
pleasure, make the most of your miles. Take along your favorite icon, your box of Kleenex, and your best kept secrets. The
guy in the next seat is only too anxious to exercise absolution
or interpretation. His credentials are impeccable. Trust me. I
sat next to him on my last flight, and I never felt better.

THE BEASTIES OF DOMESTIC BLISS

First of all, I am not paranoid. This affirmation is important because—with the exception of women whose husbands' business trips are far and frequent—readers will find that doubtful, I'm sure, by the end of this essay.

But how DO the little beasties know that he's leaving? For deep in the mechanism of every appliance, light fixture, automobile, and virus lives a molecular monster whose sole purpose is to wreak havoc simultaneously on single heads of household. Through some kind of subterranean communication channel, the word goes out: "He's gone again!" And hey presto, all hell breaks loose. The phenomenon would make a wonderful scientific study; while it might be difficult empirically to prove causation, correlation is clearly a given. Any aspiring Ph.D. candidate interested in extra-terrestrials, extra-sensory perception, or extra aggravation is certainly welcome to camp at my house. But who would want to? The place is highly contagious, and they'd have to wash their underwear by hand until next Tuesday when the appliance repairman is due. My husband, you see, left last week.

The scenario usually goes something like this: my husband announces that he's going to the hinterlands of Asia for three weeks. "Is it flu season already?" I ask. He's barely out the door when I notice that my son's cheeks are flushed. I go to the bathroom for the thermometer just in time to hear orchestral gurglings from the toilet. "Mom," my daughter bellows from the laundry room, "the washer won't work!" In the middle of the night, all the hall lights burn out with the precision of a British drill team, and at 8:00 a.m. the car is in desperate need of a post-mortem examination. I call the office to say I'll be late: I have to get the car fixed, call the appliance man, get the kids' medicine. "When did he leave?" asks my secretary.

In 17 years, I've never gotten used to this predictable phenomenon, but I've learned how to cover when my husband calls.

"Hi, Hon! How's everything?"

"Fine! Just fine! David's fever is down, there's a chance the washer may get fixed before next Tuesday, and the car will be ready tomorrow."

"Great. Glad to hear everything's okay! I miss you."

"I miss you too," I say. "More than you'll ever know." We hang up and I think about how true these words are as I crawl wearily into bed. Only a week to go until he gets back. Nothing else could possibly go wrong before then, I muse drowsily. So I drift into sleep, blissfully unaware of hovering beasties and the queasiness building up quietly in my stomach.

CHRISTMAS CRAZIES

"That's it. No other way to handle it!" declared a colleague of mine suddenly one day in early November. A gratified smile replaced the frown that had been there a moment ago.

"Difficult client?" I asked.

"No. Worse than that," she said. "Christmas." My blank stare prompted her to continue. "I'll have to go home for Thanksgiving. It's the only way to cope with Christmas."

She still wasn't making sense, but I assumed I was being dense.

"It's like this," she volunteered. "If I only go home for Christmas, it'll be a disaster. I'll anticipate it for weeks and then it won't possibly live up to my expectations and I'll get all depressed. But if I go home for Thanksgiving and stay long enough for the family to irritate me, I won't have any false ideas about Christmas and I'll be able to really enjoy it! See?"

I did, vaguely, but before either of us could further contemplate her rationale, the raised voice of a third coworker distracted us both.

"But I have to spend it with MY family," bellowed our usually meek friend into the telephone. "I always spend Christmas with my family!"

Several exchanges later, she slammed the phone down. "Men!" she uttered venomously, making off for the women's room.

Some weeks later, my own seasonal dementia struck with a vengeance. I realized I was having an annual recurrence as I pounded uncooperative cookie dough with a violence that shocked me.

"Why not skip the baking this year?" asked my husband. "The kids don't actually eat the cookies anyway."

"You can't skip the baking!" screeched my two children in unison. "It doesn't matter about eating them, only you have to bake at Christmas!"

He tried again to be supportive. "Do it next weekend."

"I can't," I muttered between clenched teeth. "Next weekend we have to cut the tree, decorate the house, shop, wrap, go to the Peace Pageant, and entertain the Smiths."

"And then can we have hot chocolate and sit in front of the fire?" asked my son. "That's what you're supposed to do at Christmas."

"According to who?" I demanded. "The Brady Bunch? Bill Cosby? Ozzie and Harriet?"

"Who's Ozzie and Harriet?" asked my daughter.

"I'm getting too old for this. Next year it's gonna be different," I declared as my husband handed me a sherry to calm me down.

"Yeah, Ma, sure. You say that every year!"

She was right, of course. Just like every year I swear that I'm not going to fuss over Christmas dinner, or spend so much on presents, or send so many cards. Either it fits or we throw it out. No Exchanges - No Returns.

But memory is kind, life is short, and Christmas is Christmas.

'Tis the season to be crazy, falalalala, lalalala.

Frustration Fugue

I t started with the Sears repairman. Nothing wrong with the lawn mower, he said. A little spit and polish and all would be right. With a self-righteous grin, he demonstrated his wisdom by starting a purring machine for my still-skeptical husband, who loaded the lawn mower into the car. He knew, he said later, just knew what would happen when he got home. Which, of course, it did. No sooner had he started up the garden path, so to speak, than the motor sputtered and died once more. Back to Sears, where my husband, who is not a mechanic but is nevertheless pretty gadget-savvy, told the guy to try again—this time paying attention to the ignition or the timer. "It couldn't be the ignition or the timer," said the smirking mechanic with a superiority inconsistent with his age or his intellect. It probably goes without saying that several months and many mechanics later, a faulty ignition was diagnosed, treated, and cured, at a relatively enormous cost in time and gray hairs.

Diagnosis, treatment, and cure was at the heart of the matter when I consulted a physician for what I felt certain was early gall bladder symptoms. "Not gall bladder," he declared emphatically, referring me to a barrage of specialists for a battery of tests, despite a set of symptoms which to my mind (and body) were clearly connected. With extraordinary skill at selective attention, each of these medical types proceeded to address my somatic complaint in segmented fashion; at no time was I perceived as a complete human by any of them. The further into this abyss I went, the more clearly I could see where it was leading me: pink pills for this, blue tablets for that, and a gothic desire for invasive diagnostics (since the insurance would pay for it). "Before this year is over," I told my husband solemnly, "someone is going to suggest I cut off my head so we can rule out brain tumor. Enough!" At this

point, I took matters into my own hands. Following my best
instincts, I consulted an acupuncturist with a refreshingly holistic
approach. "Gall bladder," he said simply, when I described
my aches and pains, which have subsided beautifully in his
care.

Next it was my car, which my husband and I can't claim
credit for diagnosing. An honest mechanic told us that our
expensive and fairly new jet-age automobile had a failed air
conditioner compressor. "This shouldn't happen in ten years,"
he said. "Your dealer should replace it." When we shared the
problem with the dealer, and pointed out that it was a rather
expensive warranty item, he rolled his eyes and looked at his
"team of experts" with charitable indulgence. "I was a mechanic
before I was a manager," he said, straightening the knot of his
necktie. "This is NOT an air conditioning compressor problem! (You can take the grease out of the monkey, but you can't
take the grease monkey out of the man.) We argued for some
time over this one, and by the end of it, much to his chagrin,
the dealer replaced the air conditioning compressor, no charge.

The point of recounting these events is simply this: Doctor,
Lawyer, Indian Chief, Medic, Mechanic, or Merchant—none
seems able to hear, let alone credit, consumers with even a
modicum of insight or intellect. Despite (or perhaps because
of) a consumer movement so powerful that it reverberates
through the entire fabric of society, service providers still seem
unable to work in partnership with their customers and clients.
What do they feel threatened with? Loss of esteem, mystique,
and in some cases, a few dollars?

Maybe the question they should be asking themselves is not
what may be lost, but rather, what can be gained by sharing
the notion of expertise with those who come to consult them.

The kids with the credentials need to stop long enough to
realize that it isn't a test of wills: we don't need to dance
around each other in a monotonous and frustrating fugue.
Instead, we can change the beat and no one even has to skip
a step. It's all a matter of trusting your partner and knowing
that whether you're following or in the lead, no one is going
to tread on your toes.

That's real harmony, and to this consumer, music to the ear.

PET PEEVES

New Years' resolutions are a good thing. Who among us will not profit from sound review and revision? We can all benefit from an annual catharsis aimed at purging our spirits of those myriad annoyances that have come to be known as pet peeves. For those of you who may have trouble getting started, or for whom this constitutes a new ritual related to ringing in the new year, allow me to offer some suggestions.

1.   Automated telephone systems: These are the wonders of technology guaranteed to ensure that at no time in any telephone transaction will you be able to actually speak to another human being. "Thank you for calling the Mettleschmertz Company," a pleasant voice of the male or female variety croons. "For information on your account, press "one" now! To report a mistake in your bill, press "two" now!" And so on. Let's say you do press "two" NOW. "If the mistake is in your favor, press "three" now! If the mistake is not in your favor, press "four" now!" And so on . . . Finally, "To have your bill mailed to you, press "five" now! To terminate this conversation, press "six" now!" To speak to a human being. . . . forget it!

2.   Frequent flyer programs: These are the bane of existence for frequent travelers trying to keep up with what originally seemed to be the only benefit of deregulation in the airlines industry a la Reagan. Designed to confuse participating travelers so that they will eventually give up using the program, thereby allowing the airlines to drop it, the announcement of benefits usually looks something like this: "Between now and May 23rd, assuming that falls on a Tuesday following a Monday holiday, you may fly one way from Dallas to Jakarta, providing it is after 6:00 p.m. our time but not before midnight their time, and there is no monsoon rain predicted. Offer good on Wednesdays only." For anyone who wonders what happens

to these copywriters, it now seems obvious that they move on to write coupon programs. Have you noticed how many grocery coupons lately offer "a head of lettuce free (up to 89 cents) if you buy four bushels of spaghetti and ten bottles of salad dressing with blue labels on Mondays. Offer expires when you read this coupon."

3. Telephone solicitations: No matter what it is they're flogging, these saccharine souls (all of whom have been previously employed recording commands for automated telephone systems) always call at the dinner hour. "Hi there! How are ya' this evening? This is Doug from your local Performing Arts Society (Read also Alma Mater, Favorite Charity, Rescue Squad). Last year you supported our capital campaign fund, and we'd like to enlist your support again this year!" Oh yeah? Well, get this Doug: Press "zero" and buzz off, NOW!

4. Mail addressed to Card Sort 123 or Resident: Mail has always been an important thing in my life. Like a ringing telephone (before the Dougs of the world invaded the wires), I can't leave it unattended. I remember the days when the mailbox promised an occasional treasure like a letter from a far-away pen pal or a package from great aunt Hattie. At the very least, people who had sent you something knew who you were. Ah, the good old days. Now, with conditioned reflex, I bound out to the box as soon as I hear the mailman and initially, I am not disappointed. A swell of paper greets me. Closer scrutiny, however, reveals four unsolicited catalogs, twelve fund raising pleas, an URGENT!! mailgram from the political party of my choice, a "personal" letter from my congresswoman (signed in the basement of the U.S. Capitol by a handwriting machine), and an update of my frequent flyer account indicating that if I buy six giant jars of mayonnaise I can enter the sweepstakes for a day in Hawaii.

5. Hyperbole in advertising: The market on this phenomenon tends to be cornered by carriers of commodities, mail, and people, and relates to the speed with which they can deliver. Airlines, for example, crow about quick service and name themselves things like Avion Express. Beware! These quick

jump special fleets (otherwise known as "commuters") are usually made up of three engine rejects from Third World countries, and flying them falls into the category of "an interesting experience." The U.S. Postal Service is another master at marketing speedy service, when we all know in reality they have only two speeds: slow and terminal.

You begin to get the picture. No doubt you are now well on your way to adding to this starter list. Unless, of course, your first pet peeve is other people's public complaining, in which case there is only one thing left to say:

Have a great new year, and may all your peeves be paltry!

EPILOGUE: A PARABLE

THE DAY VIRGINIA WENT TO THE CLUB

O nce upon a time there were three friends called Mr. Engineer, Mr. Economist, and Dr. Epidemiologist. At least that's what their clients and business partners—as well as the people who served them—called them. Sometimes even their wives referred to them that way. But they were known to each other as Chip, Buck, and Doc, nicknames that were used in direct correlation to back-and-bum slapping—the more frequent the blow, the stronger the friendship.

This tradition was most often enjoyed in the privacy of their club, Arrogants Anonymous, where they and other gentlemen came to sit in plush chairs, talk in hushed tones, eat in subdued elegance, smoke cigars, play pool, and read newspapers, spread sheets, and an occasional dirty magazine (only for the quality of the interviews, of course). In order to belong to AA, members were required to have attended certain schools, to have descended from the right paternal families, and to be worth an amount of money which whether rounded up or down had a good many zeros attached. Less easy to measure but just as important was the intellectual ability to obscure, obfuscate, obliterate, objectify, trivialize, and otherwise ignore a good bit of the world's reality, and fifty percent of its population.

AA had been providing what its members regarded as an oasis of civility and culture for more than a century, when one day something startling occurred. The event was so shocking that it left most of the members speechless for a period of time. They wandered around the cavernous chambers, hands behind their backs or clenched and shoved into pockets, puffing on cigars, until the room was so full of smoke they could hardly see the mirrors. Finally one gentleman spoke.

"Women! Absolutely not! We can't have women entering the club. What next!"

A great harumph and clearing of throats signalled consensus.

"Still, I suppose we'll have to interview her. Appearances, you know. One can't be too careful these days."

So a committee was appointed to receive the woman who had taken the startling, unprecedented, and upsetting step of applying for membership in AA. In the recesses of their minds, each committee member thought her clearly deranged. "What does the woman want, anyway?" muttered a psychiatrist member of the committee, not really expecting an answer to his rhetorical question.

Now it so happened that the woman in question, who had no male siblings, had—by what the gentlemen considered an extraordinary stroke of luck—received a sizeable inheritance which she had chosen to invest in her own education (which is partly why they thought her crazy). By what the AA members considered to be a biological fluke, she had demonstrated a superior intellect by graduating *summa cum laude* from a respected academic institution which, in their collective view, had made the irreparable mistake of admitting women. As she bore a prestigious name from her paternal lineage, the men were required to give serious consideration to her request for admission into AA.

Why, you might well ask, did this intelligent woman wish to enter such a bastion of male pride and prejudice? The answer is simply this: her superior intelligence correlated inversely with her limited tolerance of all things stupid and silly. And so she found herself needing to confront misogyny because, like Mount Everest, it was there.

Finally, the day of her interview dawned. The men on the committee, which included Chip, Buck, and Doc, assembled an hour before she was to arrive, fortifying themselves with brandy and brash witticisms. Then they seated themselves across an unraised dais and instructed that "the little lady" be brought in.

She entered the room briskly, her head cocked slightly to one side. Her dark, deep set eyes met each of their stares with an intensity that made them look at the tips of their cigars and the edge of the table. The men smiled nervously while her lips remained firm and neutral. She was a handsome figure in her tailored suit (which they would each admit later on in the privacy of the smoking room).

"Do sit down, Virginia!" said the psychiatrist, who, like his esteemed colleagues, always called women, children, and servants by their first names. It made him feel rather silly to see that she was already seated of her own accord. "Now then, what's this about wanting to join AA?"

Taking up this question in a fully prepared and impressively articulate way, their guest proceeded to reply, and upon ending her case, she said with eloquent simplicity, "You see, gentlemen, we each need what might be called metaphorically 'a room of our own,' don't you agree?"

"Yes, yes, of course," muttered the chairman. "Quite. But, well, you know, we have a tradition here, and while we concur in spirit—and by Jove, we do!—well, the fact is, that by that very tradition, well, AA has never admitted women."

"Oh, but you have!" said Virginia. The men grew pale. "You have women here. Admittedly, they do not enter the front door. They do not dine with you, or converse, or join your games. But they are here."

"Where?" demanded the gentlemen in unison. "How are they here, and at the same time invisible, tell us that!"

"How, indeed?" answered Virginia. Then she said, "The women I speak of are those who cook your meals, iron your linens, fetch your supplies, clean your toilets, wash your dishes, bake your bread—shall I go on?"

"Oh, THOSE girls!" said Chip. "The ones who make everything work!"

"But they don't count!" said Buck.

"They don't stay long either," said Doc. "Always barefoot and pregnant!" he chuckled, elbowing his neighbor, whose back and bum were inaccessible for the moment.

The gentlemen began to titter among themselves, forgetting about Virginia, who now rose to take her leave. "I shall expect your consideration in timely fashion," she said. "Good day."

"Good day," the men said in unison, shuffling their chairs like schoolboys before an exiting teacher. When she had gone, they loosened their ties, lifted their brandy snifters, and with a unified sigh, raised their glasses together—speechlessly toasting they knew not what.

For many weeks they kept silent on the issue, fervently hoping that if they ignored her, Virginia would go away. But then one day a letter arrived from her, asking for their decision. And with this letter began an epistolary debate that lasted for so long that eventually two members of the committee died; one retired from the club citing "exhaustion"; and yet another was dismissed on the grounds of incompetence, which, it was rumored, resulted from syphilitic outbreaks too frequent to overlook any longer.

In the end, Virginia was not admitted to AA, but neither did she entirely go away. Rather, she wrote and spoke and organized women and others of like mind. Ultimately, her effect was far more powerful than if the club had let her in. For she planted in the minds of many the seeds of a movement so strong that eventually it changed the course of life for just about everybody. Even those who didn't agree with her had to admit that things were never quite the same after the day Virginia went to the club. And as for Chip, Buck, Doc, and the others, well, they continued their camaraderie; but although they never knew why, it was different after that, and they felt somehow confused and cheated. "Bloody feminine mystique!" and "Damn powerful this sisterhood thing!" they were heard to mutter amongst themselves by the men who served them (for by now, women had refused to work in a club that did not admit them through the front door). Perhaps the most telling thing was that they had long since ceased patting each other's backs and bums, and in a very peculiar way, that seemed to say it all.

ORDER FORM

Books currently available from KIT:
SOURCES: An Annotated Bibliography of Women's Issues
Edited by Rita I. McCullough

A guide to the best and most recent books on women's issues. SOURCES is organized in easy-to-access categories covering subjects such as history, psychology, biography, labor, politics, health, and more. 1500 titles listed from over 160 publishers.
ISBN 1-879198-28-2 $24.95

TELLING IT LIKE IT IS: Reflections of a Not So Radical Feminist
by Elayne Clift

Real life issues as seen through a woman's eyes. This collection by an award winning writer is written with warmth, emotion, humor and insight that fully reveals the female psyche.
ISBN 1-879198-00-2 $14.95

We would like to hear from you. Write us and let us know how you liked this book. To order additional copies of this and other publications, mail a copy of this page with your check or credit card information, or call: **(203) 646-7831, Ext. 175,** or FAX: **(203) 646-3931.**

KIT KNOWLEDGE, IDEAS & TRENDS, INC.
The Positive Publisher

1131-0 Tolland Turnpike, Suite 175, Manchester, CT 06040

☐ VISA ☐ MASTERCARD   Signature _____
CARD. NO. _____
EXP. DATE _____ Phone _____

Name_____
Address_____
City/State _____ Zip _____

Please send me:	Qty	Total
Sources		
Telling It Like It Is		
(CT sales taxed at 8%) (shipping & handling: $2.50) **Total**		

If I am not completely satisfied with any book, I may return it undamaged within 60 days for a full refund.